CW00863959

Etsy

Complete Beginners Guide To Starting Your Etsy Business Empire — Sell Anything!

Veronica McKinnon

Veronica McKinnon

© Copyright 2016 - All rights reserved.

Veronica McKinnon

Disclaimer Notice:

Please note the information contained within this document is for educational and entertainment purposes only. Every attempt has been made to provide accurate, up to date and reliable complete information. No warranties of any kind are expressed or implied. Readers acknowledge that the author is not engaging in the rendering of legal, financial, medical or professional advice.

By reading this document, the reader agrees that under no circumstances are we responsible for any losses, direct or indirect, which are incurred as a result of the use of information contained within this document, including, but not limited to, — errors, omissions, or inaccuracies.

Table Of Contents

Introduction 7

Chapter 1 Getting Started 11

Tips for Choosing a User Name for Your Etsy Account 11

What Are Etsy Forums? 16

How to join an Etsy chat room 19

How to Price Your Etsy Merchandise 22

Wholesale vs. Retail 25

One-of-a-kind Items...27

How to Stay Safe on Etsy 27

What You Can't Sell on Etsy....................................31

Which services can you sell? 34

How to Collect Sales Tax on Etsy Sales........................35

Chapter 2 Starting an Etsy Business 37

You will need to create an eye catching storefront 37

Pricing Your Work for Your Etsy Business 41

Compose product photos for Etsy............................ 42

Compose titles for items on Etsy 44

Marketing your Etsy business................................ 46

Etsy Teams 50

How to set up a shop on Etsy................................52

Adding Listings 53

Payment Options..56

Billing 56

Tips for saving money and time as an Etsy Shop Owner 57

Listings Manager.. 60

How to Offer Custom Items in Your Etsy Store.................... 62

Things to consider before starting an Etsy shop 64

Chapter 3 Buying and Selling 71

Timing your Etsy post 71

Setting up payment methods on Etsy 72

Things to include in your shipping policy 75

Etsy's Seller Protection Program 77

Chapter 4 Successful Start on Etsy...79

Etsy's Do's and Don'ts.. 82

Advanced Marketing Strategies 84

Chapter 5 Growing Your Base.. 93

SEO and Etsy... 94

Chapter 6 Becoming a Social Media Guru................................109

Facebook.. 110

Twitter 114

Instagram 116

YouTube 117

Chapter 7 Getting sales 119

Images 120

Blogging...125

Social Media Images 126

Content 128

Chapter 8 Getting Featured on Etsy..139

So, how can you get featured on Etsy? 140

Conclusion...147

Introduction

First of all, I would like to thank you for choosing the book "Etsy: Everything you need to know!"

Since the beginning of time, humans have been able to "create." Whether it be something you use on a daily basis, an art project, clothing or even fixing something old that may be broken; humans have historically been known to create. Our artisanal ancestors would work tirelessly with their hands, creating goods and art in exchange for compensation. Selling their items at the local market, they would sit and wait for passersby to stop and exhibit interest. Depending on the culture, some people's only job in their community or tribe would be to create useful items for use.

In today's day and age, the desire to create is still a common one. The difference is that we now have many more mediums from which to choose. Also, we have quite a bit more technology to work with, and marketplaces such as Etsy to sell our goods and crafts. We have evolved our marketplace options way beyond the more traditional brick and mortar sale locations and methods.

This book contains all of the information that you need to know about Etsy. From how to create your Etsy account and selecting a username, to how you can collect sales tax on your sales, this book will help to guide you. So, before getting started, you will need to know a little about Etsy. Etsy can be described as a platform that connects people from all around the world, both online as well as offline, for making, buying and selling unique, antique, and homemade goods or products.

The essence of Etsy is the global community of entrepreneurs who are using Etsy for selling what they make, shoppers who are looking for unique products that can't be found elsewhere, manufacturers partnering with Etsy sellers for mutual growth and the employees of Etsy, who help in maintaining and nurturing this platform. Think of Etsy as the "artist market" of the internet, kind of like the ones you have in your local downtown on the weekends; except this is 24/7. Etsy is an online community that is solely created for the purpose of selling handcrafted and vintage goods. Most of the goods offered on this site would fall into the category of art, crafts, jewelry, housewares, artisan or baked goods and paper goods. For any item to qualify as a vintage good on Etsy, it needs to be at least 20 years old, and it includes a variety of goods like clothing, costumes, jewelry, paintings and so on. One feature that sets Etsy apart from sites like eBay is that Etsy prohibits resellers on its site.

Many artists and entrepreneurs have made their Etsy shop a success by using the tools provided on the site. They then use strategic marketing techniques by learning the ins, outs, do's, and don'ts of the Etsy market, by networking and communicating with other Etsy users an artist can now grow their marketplace faster than ever. These actions alone will not make you successful, but they can help you take a step in the right direction and bring in your first customers.

If you are a budding entrepreneur dealing in the commodities mentioned above, then Etsy is the right place for you to get started because it allows for creating a customized online shop with all the e-commerce facilities that you could possibly need. So, without further ado, let us get started. Happy reading!

Veronica McKinnon

Chapter 1
Getting Started

Tips for Choosing a User Name for Your Etsy Account

The username that you opt for on Etsy will be yours for as long as you have an Etsy account that is operational. When you decide to open up a shop on Etsy, then your username would become your shop name as well, so you will need to be careful while selecting your username. Etsy will generate two shop names depending upon your username and you get to choose one. When you are picking out a username on Etsy, make sure that you keep a few pointers in your mind. Opt for a name that is easy to remember, spell, and doesn't contain more than one or two words that are in sync with one another.

A very practical tip to keep in mind is that Etsy does not permit spaces in usernames or shop names. The easiest way to differentiate between the different words in your username and shop name, then, is to capitalize each word this will allow the name to be read more quickly, rather than customers having to read the name a few times before they pick out the words.

Some people choose to use their first and last name, first and middle name, or their first, middle, or last name as their shop's title. Either of these would work just as well, seeing as how you are the creator of the products. It's always a good idea to attach your name to your product so that people can associate your product with your name in the future. Although it isn't critical that you use your name, it certainly wouldn't be a horrible business decision. If you happen to have a following elsewhere, then you can make use of your own name as your username. While doing this, it will be difficult to retain your privacy on Etsy but it will help you capitalize on your success in the real world.

If you do not want to use your own name, then there are several tips to think about when picking the name for your shop. Consider a name that will reflect what you sell. For instance, if you specialize in customized fridge magnets then you can probably incorporate the word magnets into your username. Keep in mind, should you decide to sell create and sell something other than magnets in the future, you want to make sure your name would still be applicable so select your name carefully so that it will allow for probable expansion in the future. Suppose you have multiple user accounts on Etsy, one for each type of business that you are involved in: then you will need to disclose the alternate profiles on each of your accounts. Select a username that is representative of your style, and for legal reasons, it would be in your best interest if you can steer clear of using words that are trademarked or copyrighted.

You will also want to make sure that, aside from picking a name that is not trademarked, you pick something that is original. If your name is too similar to another shop's name, then potential customers might get confused between the two shops — and you want to make sure that your shop stands out. You can do a quick test by searching for your name ideas on the internet; if you find the same name quickly and easily, then you should probably change your username.

You also may want to think about checking on other social media sites, such as Twitter or Facebook, if you might be promoting your shop on those sites in the future; again, similarity with other users will not help to establish your originality and get your shop remembered by potential customers. Having consistency in your name between social media platforms, however, will help to get your name out there and have people remember it, so it is important to pick a username that will work across platforms if you intend to use other social media sites at all.

To help make sure that your username is original, you can choose a word or phrase that has a personal meaning to you; this will help your shop name to stand out, and will reflect who you are as a seller and creator. Or you may want to consider using words that will create a visual mental image, which might help your shop's name to better stay in people's memory.

You will also want to ensure that your username represents your style and the type of items that you will be selling. For example, if you are selling vintage or vintage-feeling items, you may want to select a username that has a vintage feel itself, or that alludes to the fact that your items are vintage.

For obvious reasons, Etsy prohibits the usage of words that are considered to be racist or profane. It is a good idea to steer away from names like this, anyway: unless you are selling racist or profane items (which again, is frowned upon on Etsy), then a name like that will not reflect you and your products anyway, and will almost certainly turn customers away.

As one last step before selecting your final username, you may want to do a quick feedback test. Ask friends, family, and especially people who would be your target market what they think of the name, and especially what they would think a shop with that name would sell if they saw it while browsing Etsy.

Even a small sampling of people can help to guide you in selecting the appropriate username.

Finally, as will be discussed in Chapter 2, keep in mind that you will also want to choose a logo and other items to help establish the brand of your Etsy shop. You may want to think about how your username will be represented by a logo before you make the final decision on what your username will be so that you are not stuck with a username that you can't properly brand.

If you have not yet officially opened your shop, then you can change your shop name as often as you would like. However, once you open your account, you can change it <u>once</u>; after that, you must submit a name change request to Etsy support, and the request may or may not be granted. Also, once you have opened the shop, your shop name is then in use and cannot be used with another account.

Another option for changing your username or shop name is to set up a new account and then migrate to it. If you have set up shop on Etsy and have established a follower base, then this can prove to be a headache. You will have to transfer items from one shop to another by hand and this means that you will need to pay the listing fees again. The other problem with changing your username would be that the sales records, customer feedback, conversations, and all the other Etsy interactions wouldn't be transferred to your new shop. Keeping your best interests in mind, choose your initial username wisely.

What Are Etsy Forums?

The member forums that are offered in Etsy let you interact with the members of the Etsy community. Etsy is a brilliant place for buying and   selling handmade and vintage goods. But Etsy is so much more than just a virtual market place; it's an online community of interesting, talented, and creative individuals.

A forum is considered to be a meeting place for the public to have open discussions. This word is derived from the system of marketplaces and public places that were present in the Roman Empire. In a similar manner, Etsy forums provide such a meeting place for all Etsy members: Etsy forums are public message boards where members can discuss any topics.

Etsy is about community, and users who participate in the forums are encouraged to treat the forums and the other participating members like fellow community members. You should be sure to be respectful and encouraging of other members, and be constructive in your suggestions and criticisms of the site.

There are moderators for the forums, who help to keep the forums and threads within the forums organized, and encourage positive and supportive interactions. A decision made by a moderator regarding inappropriate behavior will not be up for debate, so make sure that you are abiding by the rules of the forums if you participate.

Etsy supports six main forums. The first one is Announcements, which is specifically reserved for the staff at Etsy for posting any announcements that are related to the site. Users should keep checking this forum to stay informed about any upcoming changes and announcements about the site and the site's maintenance.

The second forum is Questions and, like the name suggests, this provides the answers to the general questions that the users might have regarding Etsy, basic usage, questions related to the features offered, or any other miscellaneous queries related to the policy of the site. Either someone who is a part of the Etsy community or Etsy staff will answer the questions posted on this forum.

The third forum is Discussions, and this is the go-to forum for seeking or sharing business advice. For instance, it provides information relating to running and marketing the Etsy shop, assistance with any PayPal related issues, information about shipping, or any advice related to business and business operations. There might be times when you would have come up with an idea that could revolutionize Etsy; for such moments, there's an Etsy forum for sharing your ideas. You can also discuss changes that can be made to the site or any other site-related constructive criticism. There may also be times when you are looking for advice from other shop owners or you are looking for suggestions on something business-related. Or, you can just sit back and have a fun chat with other Etsy community members about your experiences, what is happening in the world of Etsy, etc.

If you are looking to have a completely non-business-related conversation with Etsy members, then the Chitchat Forum is for you. Maybe you are looking to find people with similar interests or other local Etsy sellers with whom you might be interested in meeting up 'in real life'. If you are looking just to get away from the business side of things for a little while and have some fun and laidback conversation, then check out the Chitchat Forum.

The Promo Forum is an excellent place to promote your Etsy items and shop, and to see promotions that are being offered by other Etsy community members. Joining the Promo Forum is an excellent way to score some deals, and to get your items out to the community.

The Bugs Forum is for reporting about any bugs that you might have encountered on the site, or for checking if the other users have experienced similar glitches. You may be able to get some assistance from other community members about how they have dealt with similar problems, or recommendations as to possible solutions that you could try out. You can make use of this forum to report such glitches as well, but remember that none of the forums on Etsy are complaint desks; if you need to file a complaint or a grievance then you can email it to community@etsy.com. That way you can be sure that the Etsy support team will see and address your concerns.

How to join an Etsy chat room

The good news is that on top of offering forums, Etsy also hosts various chat rooms that you can make use of for interacting with other members. For instance, you might want to join chats that are being organized by your favorite Etsy team's captain. If there isn't a chat room that caters to your specific needs, then you can always start a new one.

For accessing other Etsy chatters, you need to open the main Etsy Community page. Now, click on the Chat link that is present in the top-center of the page. When the Chat Room pages open, they display the list of chat rooms that are currently active and there's also the option for you to create a new chat room according to your specifications. If you want to join a chat room that is already active, then in the Chat Rooms page you just need to click on the Join button that's placed next to the entry for the chat room that you want to enter. If the chat that you want to join is password enabled, and then you will see a field that has a lock option for joining the chat, you will need to type in the password and you will be able to enter the chat room. If you don't have the password, you will be unable to join or enter the chat room. Locked chatrooms are used for matters not open to the general public, or matters that are specific to a certain category.

Every Etsy chat room, regardless of it being a new or an existing one, has a similar layout. On the left side of the screen, you will be able to see lines of text that are scrolling upwards with a name beside it. These lines of text are the conversation going on in the chat room and the corresponding name is of the user who typed it. For adding your own opinions to the chat, you need to type in the Chat field and then hit Enter or Send.

The right side of the chat has images and these are the images that have been shared in the chat regarding various listings as well as the links to those listings. A smaller image would show the avatar of the user who shared the listing. If you want to share your own item or listing, you can copy the listing ID or the URL and paste it in the field below the scrolling images and hit send or enter. You can share photos from any listing and not just your own. The thumbnail sized images that are present below all the item listings, are the avatars of the Etsy users who put the listings in the chat. Pointing the pointer over the picture will display their Etsy Shop, Profile and message links.

Creating a new chat room is as simple as joining a new one. At the bottom of the Chat Rooms page, you will need to simply type in the name of the new chat room that you want to create under the Create New Room option. You can either opt for creating a password for it to keep it private or you can leave it open to the public. So, type in the password to protect the chat in the Password field. You can send the same password to the other Etsy users via a personal conversation. Now you need to click the option Create to create your desired chat room. You cannot close the chat room that you have opened, but the chat room will disappear from the list of chats that are active if it has been continuously inactive for a particular period of time.

The more traffic that a chat room receives, the higher up it will appear on the list. What's also interesting about the chat rooms is that they are not only for business and shop related issues, they are also for everyday conversations. People start discussions about posting pet pictures and celebrity rumors; it's a way to keep you connected with artisans like yourself. Due to the majority of Etsy full timers that work from home, sometimes you can begin to feel isolated and lonely — having these chat rooms allows for some interaction outside of your home.

How to Price Your Etsy Merchandise

When you start selling your products or goods in your Etsy store, you probably wonder about the amount you should charge the customers for your items. If you want to have a profitable Etsy shop, then you will need to be comfortable going over some numbers and doing a little math regarding your pricing strategy. There are two simple formulae that you will need to learn for this and they aren't difficult.

The first one is **(Materials+Labor+Overhead) X2 = Wholesale price** and the second one is **Wholesale price X2 = Retail price.** Offering your items at different price points by making use of the above formulae will help you spread your customer base. For instance, you specialize in ceramic items, then you might sell the ceramic mugs at different price points depending upon whether they are small, medium or large and in a similar fashion you can have ceramic bowls that come in varying sizes and different price ranges. By doing this you will be catering to a wider audience and increasing the number of potential buyers.

Calculating the cost of materials:

When you start calculating the cost for materials; you will need to include every single component that's related to your item. For instance, let us assume that you sell handmade soft toys for children. You will need to include the cost of all the material cost that is required for the finished product. You will need to take into consideration the fabric, rickrack, label, stuffing or thread and anything else that you might need for making the final product. When you are calculating the cost of the materials you use then you will need to consider the price of the product that you have used in one piece. You might have purchased 3 yards of fabric for $12, but if it takes only about one third of it for a single piece then the cost of fabric per piece would be $4.

The same goes for jewelry making. Taking into account the cost of materials, stones, wiring, clasps — along with the cost of labor and packaging — your pricing needs to be set at a point where your costs to make the item are covered and you are profiting. No business ever stayed afloat not making a profit.

Calculating the labor costs:

For calculating the labor costs that are involved for producing one single piece, you will need to set your labor costs on an hourly basis. While you are doing this, you need to make sure that you are paying yourself a fair wage for the amount of work that you have put in and the level of skill involved. This consideration will be extremely important if you are looking forward to quitting your day job. Many of the professional crafters usually set the labor cost between $12 and $20 per hour depending on the trade. If you are just starting out, then you might want to start off with a lower rate. You can keep giving yourself periodic increments depending upon the improvement in your skills.

If you know your labor costs, then you can start working out your labor costs. This cost needs to take into consideration the factors like time taken for designing a piece, shopping for supplies, completing the piece, photographing it, creating an item listing, and then packaging as well as shipping the item. If you end up clearing more than $400 from your Etsy shop in a year, then you will have to pay sales tax at the rate of around 30%. All of these factors need to be taken into consideration when attempting to set a price on your items because, as I said before, you need to be able to profit after you have paid your costs.

Adding up overhead:

It is not just about calculating the cost of labor and material involved; you need to take into account the overhead costs as well. The overhead would include the tools and equipment required in the manufacturing of the product, office supplies, packaging material, utilities like electricity, internet etc., used, fees paid towards PayPal and Etsy and so on. The shipping costs aren't included in this. So, you will need to calculate the shipping costs separately and then pass them along to the buyer.

Overhead also includes any items that you make multiples of; for example, say you create throw pillows: one particular pillow seemed to sell well, so you produced ten to keep as inventory so that once they were ordered, you could ship them off. The only problem with this overhead is if the pillows stop selling, you are going to have ten throw pillows and ten throw pillows worth of materials sitting around. Ideally, items should be made to order to avoid this overhead; however, this is not always possible. In the formulae that were mentioned above, after adding the material costs, labor costs and overhead costs, you will need to multiply the resultant sum by 2. The final number times two will be your profit. This is the amount that you will need to invest in your business again. If there are any repairs to any of the machines you use or any maintenance costs, you can make use of this amount for meeting those expenses.

Wholesale vs. Retail

It is helpful to determine two prices for the items that you are selling: the wholesale price, and the retail price. Retail is for customers who purchase individual pieces, whereas wholesale is for customers who buy your items in bulk.

While wholesale pricing is often intended for customers who may be reselling your items, it is helpful even if you are not going to be selling to customers for that purpose. If you make items that might be purchased in bulk by a customer for a special event, it will be useful to have a wholesale price pre-determined. For example, if you make decorations and a customer wants to purchase several decorations for an upcoming wedding, then you are most likely going to offer a wholesale price so as to encourage the larger purchase. Having the price pre-determined makes it easier for you when the request comes in, and it also may provide an incentive to customers if they can see that information on your shop page and so know that they will be getting a deal if they buy in bulk.

Having a wholesale price figured out is also useful in guiding you on what your sale price might be for items, if you choose to run a sale. Sales can promote your items to customers and encourage them to visit your shop. A wholesale price is usually at least a good starting point for determining a sale price because you will have already figured out your overhead so that you know how much you can reduce your price and still make a profit, especially if you sell a certain number of the sale items.

One-of-a-kind Items

One last consideration when determining the price of your items is whether they are one-of-a-kind items, or whether you are creating multiple similar items. If each item is unique, this will usually justify a higher price than if the same piece can be purchased by multiple customers. If you do price according to the uniqueness of your items, though, make sure that they are unique, and that you are not selling items that are too similar to different customers. Otherwise, you will likely get some very negative feedback if customers start to figure out that they are paying for unique items that are not unique!

How to Stay Safe on Etsy

One of the main features of Etsy is the community of interesting and creative people that it thrives on. But there might be instances when you have a not so pleasant encounter with the other members. Like with any other online platform there are certain precautions that you will need to take even on Etsy.

To ensure that no one accesses your account without your authorization, you will need a strong password. For having a strong password there are certain conditions, it needs to be at least eight characters, shouldn't contain your real name or your username, is not a complete word, differs from the previous passwords that you have made use of and it should be a mix of uppercase letters, lowercase letters, symbols, numbers and spaces as well. You can also keep changing your password after every 90 days to make sure that you have an added layer of protection.

Stay alert and lookout for scams. These scams often involve payment made in the form of cashier's checks, money orders, a significant sum of money to pay towards shipping costs that's more than necessary or any other charge that seems unusual.

Another common scam involves the buyer asking you to ship the item to an address that is different from the one in their Etsy or PayPal account. The buyer ends up not receiving the item, and you will have to provide a refund for the cost because you sent it to an address that is different than what the buyer has <u>officially</u> given. If you refuse to comply, the buyer may threaten to leave negative feedback about you and your store, which could, of course, impact your business reputation and prevent other buyers from being willing to purchase your products. Pay very close attention to the wording in the requests, as there tends to be a frequent misuse of grammar and transitions. It is better to be safe than sorry in any instance, so never comply with any requests that you find to be odd, generous, or excessive, as these may be attempts to scam.

Remember that Etsy will never send you an email asking for your password; if you receive an email like this or a similarly odd-seeming email from Etsy, then make sure to contact Etsy's customer service to let them know about the email.

If you do get scammed on Etsy, you will have to contact your financial institution, report the same to Etsy, and you can also alert your local law enforcement about it. It would also be wise to check the Etsy forums or discussions to see if anyone else has experienced or encountered the same customer. If not, start a new discussion after contacting Etsy, making others aware of the potential scam. However, in the event you are incorrect about the scam, there could be negative repercussions. Do not post on the forum unless you are sure a scam is taking place; otherwise, it's best kept to yourself.

Before jumping into any forum or a discussion, it would be better if you monitor the discussions taking place in it for a while. See the topic of discussion and the nature of the conversation, if you think the conversation is taking a turn for the worse, and then all you need to do is simply disengage. You don't need to embroil yourself in any unnecessary controversies.

To provide extra protection for its users, Etsy also offers the option of Two-Factor Authentication. If you choose to use this additional security measure, then you provide a phone number to Etsy so that Etsy can send you a code for signing in. Every time that you sign in on a new browser, or if it has been more than thirty days since you have signed in, Etsy will text or call you (depending on the option that you chose) with the new code.

When you sign up for the Two-Factor Authentication option, Etsy will also provide you with backup codes that you can use if you don't have your phone with you when you are signing in. If you lose these codes or use them up, then you can obtain new codes through your security settings options on the Etsy website.

Regarding selling your items, if you happen to be in a situation where you are meeting someone in person to sell an item, and you don't have a brick and mortar store where you can meet, then make sure to choose a public place. Tell a friend or family member what you are doing, so that someone knows where you are and when you will be returning. Do not ever meet a customer at your home, unless you know and are comfortable with the person.

One last thing that you need to keep in mind is that you shouldn't hand out your contact number or any other personal details, like your home or office address. Even details regarding different payment accounts, past customers, plans for the future of your business, or any other information in excess. Don't share any information that you wouldn't normally share on any other social networking platform. Your personal safety is in your hands, so stay safe!

What You Can't Sell on Etsy

Prohibited Items

Etsy is a marketplace of handmade goods, vintage goods and supplies. You might naturally assume that if any item you want to sell falls into one of these categories, and then you can go ahead and sell it on Etsy; however this is far from the case. So, don't form any premature assumptions. There are some items that are prohibited on Etsy.

There might be a number of items that would fall within the criteria that's been mentioned above, but their sale is prohibited on Etsy because it might be illegal, against public morality or the local laws. The list of prohibited items includes medical drugs, alcohol, narcotics and drug related paraphernalia, and substances that have or claim to have an intoxicating or healing effect. Some items that are related to the above prohibited items, but are permitted to be sold, include beer brewing kits, baked goods that contain alcohol, pipes made for tobacco consumption, and products made out of alcohol bottles.

Other items that are prohibited include firearms and other weapons, hazardous materials like flammable, corrosive, poisonous and explosive substances; exceptions to this are items like cooking knives and toy weapons.

Etsy also prohibits the sale of live animals or any other illegal animal products, and human remains or body parts. Obvious exceptions to this rule include native American crafts, non-ivory bone and antler products, leather goods, and textiles made from animal hair – it is a good thing that this last exception is allowed, or there would be some very unhappy knitters and crocheters!

Finally, the prohibited list also includes motor vehicles, pornography of any sort, real estate, as well as any recalled items. Apart from this, Etsy also prohibits the sale of such items that would facilitate in promoting discrimination on any of the grounds like sexual, racial, ethnic or so on, would promote illegal activities or harmful acts and behavior. Products that have a certain historical value, especially if used in a peaceful or religious way, will likely be permitted.

Etsy works to balance supporting a positive community that abides by all relevant laws and regulations, with encouraging artistic values and freedom of expression. The website's administrators have carefully considered which items will be permitted and which will not based on this balance.

If you have questions about whether an item of yours will be permitted to be sold on Etsy, it is safest to contact Etsy's customer support first before placing the item for sale on the website. If you place it up for sale without checking, and the item is reported to Etsy or Etsy's administrator's discover the item, your selling privileges could potentially be suspended, or even terminated.

Category Restrictions

Etsy also has restrictions on the type of items that can be sold in certain categories on the website. For example, if you are selling your items under the 'Handmade' category, then you must be either designing your items or making them yourself or both. Etsy may require you to establish your 'authorship' of the items, which may involve telling Etsy about your manufacturing process, or what tools, equipment, or materials you use to produce your items.

Production and Manufacturing Restrictions

If you partner with an outside manufacturer to produce your items, then Etsy may require certain additional information, including the manufacturer's production process, what equipment the manufacturer uses, and whether your manufacturer complies with Etsy's Ethical Expectations policy. Etsy also requires that each seller is transparent about their handmade items, including who is involved in the manufacturing process.

If Etsy contacts you with concerns or questions about your items, make sure to respond promptly and honestly. At the end of the day, Etsy has the final say as to whether your items and your shop can continue on the website, so it is best to cooperate and make sure that you are in compliance with all of Etsy's relevant policies and requirements.

Which services can you sell?

You cannot sell services on Etsy because Etsy is not a site focused on providing services to individuals; therefore making an account gauged at offering services would be difficult. You would also be unable to market yourself efficiently on Etsy because there are no service categories in which to place services for sale.

Also, Etsy is a marketplace for goods, so you cannot sell services of any form on Etsy. You cannot advertise about your business on Etsy and you aren't even permitted to avail members who are seeking particular skills related to tailoring, restoration of antiques, retouching photographs and so on. But, you can sell services that result in the creation of a new tangible item, like a graphic designer offering services for designing a logo for the client or conducting workshops, but the only precondition is that it needs to involve the production or creation of a new physical object.

How to Collect Sales Tax on Etsy Sales

You will need to collect sales tax on your Etsy sales unless you happen to reside in one of the five sales-tax free states and these are Alaska, Oregon, Delaware, New Hampshire and Montana. Specifically, you will need to collect tax on most of the goods and some of the services that you provide to a customer residing in the U.S. state where you have the physical presence of your business or a nexus, because the sales tax is based on the location from which the item is being shipped. For instance, if you are running your Etsy shop in Bangor and your customer resides in Maine then you will need to collect sales tax from such a person. But if your customer resides in Boston, then you both are off the hook.

The rate of sales tax varies from one state to the other, as well as there are some cities, countries and jurisdictions that impose sales tax that's more than the state rate. You will need to look up the rate of sales tax online so that you charge the right amount. You will need to check the state requirements of sales tax, the rate to be charged, how to register for a sales tax permit and the manner of collecting and remitting sales tax you've collected.

Not all items sold on Etsy will be taxable; if you want to find out whether your items are taxable, Etsy does provide links where you can research state-specific information.

You have the option of setting up your Etsy account for automatically collecting sales tax during checkout. When you opt for this, the sales tax will be automatically calculated by Etsy, depending upon the region that is specified by the buyers. Remember that if a customer applies a coupon code to their purchase, then the tax will be calculated from the discounted price, not the original price. For accessing these settings, you will need to click on the Your Shop option and click on the shipping and payment link within this. When this tab opens, click on the sales tax tab. For keeping track of the sales tax you have collected, you can also make use of apps that would link themselves to the Etsy account like Outright. Once you have collected all the money due towards sales tax, you will just have to make a check for the same when the payment becomes due. Keep in mind that you must obtain a sales tax ID number from your state, to report your sales tax.

Chapter 2

Starting an Etsy Business

If you are looking for a platform for channeling your passion for crafts and artistic creations into a viable business, then you can consider selling and marketing your work on Etsy. If your business can take off, then you can quit your day job and keep doing what you enjoy for earning your livelihood.

If you have always dreamed of owning your own craft business or selling items and products that you make, then opening an Etsy shop is for you. The business of Etsy can be as busy or as calm as you make it, it all depends on the products, quantities, and detail offered. If you are a creative individual, then creating your own business through Etsy can be highly rewarding and profitable if done right.

You will need to create an eye catching storefront

Your Etsy storefront is sort of the main page for your shop, where buyers can go to check out a variety of your items all at once, look at any policies that you might have in place, see items that you have sold previously, etc. There are number of ways in which you can personalize your storefront on Etsy. This personalization is of great importance to ensure that your store stands apart from the rest so that you can grab the attention of potential customers and promote your brand.

You can add a banner to your storefront. A banner is a graphic that would run across the page of your store and you can create this without much difficulty by making use of graphic software and programs like Picasa, Photoshop, and Windows Paint and so on.

Avoid using pictures you find on the Internet as your logo or banner unless you own the rights to the photos, as this can cause issues with copyright and trademark laws. It is sometimes a good idea to dish out a small amount of money to a graphic design student to have them create a logo for you. Students can be useful resources because they are learning, charge lower rates, and you can usually find them through word of mouth. Make sure to clarify any copyright issues with anyone who is designing a logo, banner, etc. for you.

Always include a shop title and shop announcement. Your shop title would be similar to a tagline and it would sum up in brief what your shop is all about. Shop announcement is different from a shop title, this would be appearing below the banner, providing information about the products you sell, the materials used and your artistic philosophy, if any exists. Your shop announcement can also be made use of for broadcasting about any upcoming sale or can be made use of for sharing your Etsy shop policies. Some people give creative, witty sentences that give a general overview of the products they offer or about the store owner. If using a catchphrase, always check to make sure it has not been used somewhere else before; otherwise, just like with copying photos from the internet, you might run into copyright issues.

You can make use of different sections for organizing the goods you sell. There are different types of items that you might sell. If you are selling products like notebooks, magnets, pens, picture frames then you can organize this as stationery and you can make use of further sections like size, type, material or price to act as filters.

Your avatar is your profile picture; ensure that you are selecting such a picture that would represent what you are doing and what your store is all about. It needs to reflect your personality and your store's character. Do not place a product as a profile picture, even if the product is still available for purchase. A lot of times, store owners will use their picture as their avatar; this gives the purchaser a more personalized feel when buying.

Try and maintain a general feel throughout the shop, anything to contrasting might put off buyers. If you decide to use a profile picture, make sure it is a clear, professional-looking photograph. Never place pornography, illicit drugs or substances, or anything else that is illegal or prohibited by Etsy as your profile picture. Your Etsy profile is a business profile so you should approach it as if you are going on a virtual interview for every customer that visits your site.

In addition to your profile picture, you also need to create your profile. If your profile is well done, it will give potential customers a clear idea of who you are, what you are selling, and why they should buy from you as opposed to another shop. Make sure that your profile has enough information about you so that prospective buyers can relate to you and want to give you their business, but not so much that it becomes unprofessional.

You should also keep in mind that if you have more than one username on Etsy, you are required to list all of your usernames in your profile. Also, if more than one person is involved in running your shop, then each person must be listed in the profile with a description as to how each person is involved in the store.

Finally, always remember that all photographs, information, and other content on your shop's site must be in compliance with Etsy's policies, including the store policies. Carefully review all of the relevant policies before you make your content available to the public, so that you avoid any disciplinary action by Etsy.

Pricing Your Work for Your Etsy Business

When you start selling your products or goods in your Etsy shop, you probably wonder about the amount you should charge the customers for your items. If you want to have a profitable Etsy shop, then you will need to be comfortable going over some numbers and doing a little math regarding your pricing strategy. There are two simple formulae that you will need to learn for this and they aren't difficult.

The first one is **(Materials+Labor+Overhead) X2 = Wholesale price** and the second one is **Wholesale price X2 = Retail price**. But the cost for shipping isn't included in this. The second formula can be adjusted according to your convenience. When you multiply the wholesale price by 2, it would provide the retail price. At times the sellers opt for a number higher than 2 like 2.5 or 3 for determining their retail price, provided that the market is willing to bear such an expense.

Compose product photos for Etsy

Product photos that are well photographed can act as a catalyst for promoting sales for your Etsy shop, but you needn't hire a professional photographer for doing this. You can very well compose your own photos, here are some pointers that will help you portray your product in the best possible manner. All you need is a little bit of artistic flair, some patience and the following guidelines. You should angle your camera; this means that tilting the camera a little so that it would put the subject matter slightly off center and create some movement and flow. This would produce a picture that is more intriguing.

Make sure that you fill the frame with your product so that it not only seems more appealing but the potential buyers can also see how well crafted your product is. For highlighting your piece dramatically and adding a little bit of panache to it, you can blur the background so that the focus automatically shifts to your product. Always frame your picture with a darker element. You can group your products together, especially if you are into designing or creating itsy bitsy products, then for attracting attention you can group several products together so that the buyer can see how cohesive your products are together. On the other hand, if you are photographing larger items, try to choose a background that will complement the item, such as a nature scene or interesting architecture. Larger items do not require that the focus is on them as much as small items do, so use the background to really sell the item.

Make use of the rule of thirds. This is a very simple rule, you will need to divide the scene that you are photographing into nine parts by making use of two horizontal and vertical lines similar to a tic-tac-toe grid. This will help in piquing the interest of the viewer. If possible, if the product contains multiple colors, aim for a background or surface that is a solid color or white; this helps give the eyes a focal point and make the product more attractive to the buyer. Always avoid loud patterned or cluttered backgrounds when possible, as these can detract from your product.

Try to avoid direct sunlight or harsh indoor light, as this can detract from the appearance of your products. Soft, natural lighting will be best for highlighting your item. Never use your camera flash, as this will be too severe.

If you are selling products that are to be worn, try to use models. If you look at any successful clothing website, there will always be a photograph of each clothing item being worn by a model. It can be very difficult for potential buyers to assess whether a product is something that would work for them when it is sitting on a hanger or draped over a flat surface. Seeing the product on a live model can make all of the difference. Also, if you use a model that makes the product look as good as possible, then this will make potential buyers more likely to purchase the product.

Remember that Etsy allows you to have a main photo as well as four additional photos for each item, so try to take a variety of photos from different angles, using various backgrounds, etc. Use the advantage of being allowed to post multiple photos to make sure that you are capturing your item in ways that will appeal to multiple potential customers and will sell your item. When choosing the main photo for your item, make sure to pick the photo that either best displays the item, or is most likely to capture a potential buyer's eye — preferably, the photo will do both.

Compose titles for items on Etsy

An item title would be similar to a good headline for a product on Etsy and it needs to be designed in such a manner that it would grab the buyer's attention and get them to want to read more about that particular item. There are a couple of guidelines that you can keep in mind that for composing a catchy title. You will need to keep it short and contain it to within 140 characters inclusive of spaces. Describe the items in the beginning of the item title so that it would help in improving the chances of searching for a particular item on Etsy. You can make use of puns; this is the time for you to get creative with words. Make use of strong words and avoid using vague vocabulary. The reader should want to read more about your product and not get confused. You can make use of uppercase and lowercase words but making use of too many uppercase words just seems like shouting. Etsy has restrictions on characters that may be used in a title as well: certain characters can only be used a limited time in each title, and other characters, including the dollar sign ("$"), are not permitted at all.

It is important to use only, or at least mostly, words that will likely be searched for by potential customers; the title is used primarily for searches, so you want to make sure that your title will show up in a search for similar products. The first few words of your title are the words that will most influence whether your product shows up in an Etsy search, so make sure to place the most descriptive, identifying, and searchable words there. If you want to give a further explanation of what the product is, or if you have a name for your product (e.g. for artwork), you can put that kind of information in your product description. It should not go in the product title because potential buyers are unlikely to be searching for those specific words.

There are questions that you can ask yourself, to make sure that you are choosing the words that will have your product showing up in an Etsy search. Ask yourself exactly what the item is, then get more specific. For example, a necklace can be described more precisely by calling it a choker necklace. If your item has a target market, put that in the title; if it is for dogs, including the word 'dog' will have your product showing up in searches for items for dogs. You may also want to consider including the primary material, especially if that is a particular selling feature of the product; this also applies to the production process, if there is something special about how the item was manufactured. Size might be significant, especially if it is for a niche size, or for clothing. If the item is intended for a specific occasion, such as a holiday, birthday, or another life event, then that is a very useful thing to include in the product title. All of these questions and more can help you to identify what you want to include in your product title, to ensure that your product shows up in relevant Etsy searches.

Marketing your Etsy business

Etsy understands the importance of marketing for the development of your business and this is the reason why it comes with several built-in promotional tools like widgets and coupon codes. Marketing and promoting your items will be very easy on Etsy if you make the best use of the following features. You should create coupon codes for your shop. Coupons will help in increasing awareness about your brand and also provides the necessary reward for them to try out your store. This will help in not only capturing the attention of your potential customers but also improves the chances of their making a sale. You can manage to steer people away from other sites by creating widgets. You can also promote your shop on various social media platforms by connecting with your friends, family and fans as well. Etsy Search Ad is a paid advertisement spot that would appear at the top of the search results page when a specific keyword is made use of.

As we talked about above, make sure that the photos that you have used to showcase your products capture the attention of potential buyers and show your products in their best light possible.

Developing your unique brand can go a long way toward increasing your sales as well. While it might be tempting to make your brand similar to that of another successful shop, at the end of the day it could backfire on you. You are more likely to be successful if you build your special brand that customers will learn to identify as having high-quality products that they want to buy.

Social media can be an online vendor's best friend, especially when it comes to building your brand. As we talked about in the previous chapter, you want to make sure that your brand is consistent across any social media platforms that you use. Whether it is Facebook, Twitter, Instagram, Pinterest or another social media platform, make sure that both your image and your message stay the same. Make sure that they highlight your products and your shop and encourage people to visit and purchase items. If you are very comfortable using the different social media platforms, you may decide to use them all, or at least several. If you are less comfortable, it is probably a good idea to pick one or two and focus on using them properly and to the fullest extent. It is better to be really great at one or two platforms then to be inconsistent on all of them.

Another possibility for building your business is to do some guest blogging. Guest blogging is where you write articles for someone else's blog (at their request, of course!). For example, you could create a brief and easy article about how to create a basic version of a product that you sell; then at the end of the article, you could include a link to your shop where you sell a more advanced (and professional-looking) version of the item. Guest blogging can have a few positive outcomes: you expand your community of support for your shop, you increase the number of links for your shop which helps with Search Engine Optimization (discussed more in Chapter 4), and you potentially raise the number of views of your site.

You may also want to consider starting your own blog, as it will not only allow you to talk about your products and your Etsy shop, but you will also be able to put links on your blog to your

Etsy shop. This will help to direct potential customers to your shop, and will also assist with Search Engine Optimization as discussed in Chapter 4.

Customer service is another excellent way in which to market your business. The more customers that are satisfied with your products and the service that your shop provides, the more they will talk about your shop and your products and encourage others to buy from you as well. The importance of providing satisfactory customer service cannot be emphasized strongly enough, especially for an online site that includes customer forums — you can be sure that if a customer is not satisfied, it will likely come up in the forums at some point.

As simple as it sounds, packaging can have an enormous impact on the likelihood of a customer coming back to purchase more items. If a customer receives your product in packaging that is fun, or exciting, or encompasses a special feeling or mood that you want your products to convey, then the experience of opening up the package and seeing the product for the first time will be even better. And as above, a happy customer is a customer who will return to your store, and who will encourage others to buy your products as well; it's a win-win situation!

Also, do not forget about in-person marketing and advertising. Even if all of your actual selling is done online, the people who are buying your products are out there in the 'real world', and every interpersonal interaction that you have is a potential customer. Invest in business cards that you can hand out to anyone who you think might be interested in your product; you can also leave them in businesses and other areas that allow that type of advertising. Flyers may also be a useful tool, especially if you can find businesses that are related to the type of product that you sell. For example, if you sell knitted products, then a brick and mortar knitting shop might be a great place to advertise your Etsy shop.

Finally, you might want to consider sending samples of your product to certain influential members of the Etsy community, or the larger online community, such as bloggers. Choose people who are likely to have a particular attraction to your products, so that you will receive the best response possible. For example, if you sell feminist-themed items, then sending some samples to a feminist blogger would probably get you some very positive feedback. If the person likes your product, they may end up writing about it online, which can be an excellent way to get the word out and increase business for your store.

Etsy Teams

Etsy teams are a great resource for sellers. There are many different teams, each specialized for a certain type of group;

whether based on location, target market, type of product, materials used, etc., there will almost certainly be a team for each type of unique factor.

It is essential to choose a team (or teams) that fit with you and your store, and that will help you to get the most out of the team experience. You can search the list of teams to find one that would suit your needs; while you can look by the type of team, you can also search by topics that they might discuss, including certain business topics that you might need help with.

Within each team's page, there will be multiple threads dealing with a variety of issues. You can browse these threads to see if there is anything of use to you, and that might help in your decision of whether to join that team. Some teams are private, which means that you will need to ask for permission to join.

If all else fails and you can't find a team that's what you're looking for, you can always start your own. It is possible that there are other Etsy sellers who are interested in the same thing as you, or who have the same problem, but no team has been created yet that addresses the issue.

Teams are great not only for seeking advice and getting the word out about your shop and your products, but it also creates a community of support. Team members will often discuss and promote each other's shops, especially if they're not direct competitors.

How to set up a shop on Etsy

Becoming a seller on Etsy is very simple and you need to just set up your shop and list the items that you are dealing in. Before getting started with this, you should make sure that you have gone through the list of items that are prohibited to make sure that the items or services you are offering don't fall in that category.

You will need to click on the Sell link that appears on the upper left corner of the page and the sell page will appear. This page contains the list of items that you can and cannot sell or offer on Etsy. Now you need to click the link that says Open an Etsy Shop. When you do this, Etsy will automatically prompt you for selecting a language, country and currency. The default currency is U.S. and the default currency is dollar because most of the Etsy users happen to be based in U.S. But this doesn't mean that individuals residing in other countries can't register on Etsy. Etsy supports 20 odd currencies and different international regions.

If you set the language of your shop as English, the currency as U.S. dollar and the country as United States, then you will need to click yes if all the information filled is up to your requirement.

If not, then you can click on the Choose link and make the necessary changes. Once you have made the changes, Etsy will save them and prompt you to select a shop name. You will have to type out the name that you want your shop to have and save all the changes. The name you have chosen for your shop will be assigned by Etsy, provided that it isn't already taken by someone else.

Adding Listings

Once you have opened the store, you will need to stock it! As we discussed above, you will need to upload photos of your items, pick a title for each item, and create a description for the product.

In addition to those steps, you will also need to determine the category in which each item should be placed. Possible categories include Accessories, Clothing, Home & Living, Shoes, Jewelry, and many others. Each category will also have a subcategory that you will have to select. When choosing your product's category, make sure to consider the most appropriate one, as buyers often search by category.

After you have chosen the category, you will have to put in information about any outside manufacturers that you use, the price of each item, and the tax to be charged. You can list the quantity that you have available for the item as well, and whether the item is a physical item or a digital one. You can also include any variations of the item; for example, if the item comes in different sizes, colors, or materials. If this is not applicable to your item, you can just skip this part.

You can also choose your renewal option for each listing. Items can stay listed on your shop for four months before they need to be renewed; you can select whether you will manually renew each item, or whether it should renew automatically.

Next, you will need to decide what shipping options you will offer for your item. You can select which countries you are willing to ship it to. You will need to click on the Sell link that appears on the upper left corner of the page and the sell page will appear — the decision is entirely yours. In this section, you will have to specify the processing time that the item will take, between when the item is ordered and when it is shipped, and what the shipping costs will be. You can choose to offer a combined shipping amount if a buyer purchases more than one item from you, which can be a great incentive for buyers.

Finally, you need to determine your search terms. Titles were discussed earlier in this book, and are an important consideration, but tags are also very useful for helping your item to be found in a search. Tags are essentially keywords that describe your product. As with titles, you should use words that describe your product and that you think potential buyers are likely to use in a search, to improve the chances of your product being found.

In addition to the tags, you will also be able to pick any materials that you want to use for search terms. If your product is of a material that will be particularly attractive to buyers for that kind of product (for example, items made out of pure wool instead of synthetic), this can be a useful tool. You can also specify the intended market (e.g. children, pets), occasion, and style. You will be limited in the amount of each of these that you can use: you can only pick one intended recipient, one target occasion, and two styles that best describe your product — so choose carefully!

Once you have entered all of this information, you are ready to publish your listing. Once you hit the 'Publish' button, your product is live, and potential buyers can see it, so take the time to ensure that all of the information is exactly as you want it. You can always edit it later, but when possible you want to avoid publishing (even temporarily) any incorrect information or anything that will prevent buyers from finding and wanting to purchase your items.

Veronica McKinnon

Payment Options

Deciding how payment will work in your shop is a very important step in setting up your store. You will need to select which payment methods you will accept. Etsy offers direct checkout, which you will be required to use if you are in a country where it's available. The Direct Checkout option is only available in certain countries (primarily the United States, Canada, and European countries), so you should check Etsy's list to make sure that it is available to you. The Direct Checkout method allows a buyer to pay by credit/debit, PayPal, gift cards, and a few other ways that are more country-specific.

If you are located in a country where Direct Checkout is not available, you still have a few options: you can use your PayPal account, check or money order ("payment by mail"), or you can determine a different method. If you do choose a different method, make sure to check all of Etsy's relevant policies, as well as any applicable laws in your location, to make sure that you are in compliance.

Billing

In addition to figuring out how you will be paid by buyers, you will also need to choose how you will pay Etsy for the fee to sell on the website. Depending on the country where you're located, you may be required to use a credit card to open your shop. The credit cards accepted by Etsy are Visa, MasterCard, American Express, Discover, and Carte Bleue in France. Debit cards with these logos should work as well. Also, for sellers in certain countries, Etsy may ask you to keep a credit card on file in order to verify your identity. These requirements do not apply to sellers in Austria, Germany, or the Netherlands.

While you may need to provide your credit card information to open the account or verify your identity, you do not have to pay for your Etsy account using a credit card. You can choose to pay by using PayPal instead if that works better for you. You may also be able to open your shop using your PayPal account instead of a credit card; if this available in your country, an "Authorize PayPal Account" button will show up when you are going through the process to set up billing.

Tips for saving money and time as an Etsy Shop Owner

Time is money; it's a cliché but nevertheless true, especially when you are running your own business. In this section we will take a look at the ten tips that will help you in saving money as well as time for your Etsy shop.

You can end up saving a lot of time as well as money if you can plan well in advance about the purchases you need to make. You don't have to wait till you run out of your supplies to go shopping because such emergency trips will unnecessarily increase your costs; instead make a list beforehand itself and you can also shop during sales and you can also make use of coupons to save some money and effort. Buy in bulk whenever you can. Your local office supply store might be very convenient due to its proximity, but the purchases made from it are definitely going to be gouging into your profits. You can save a chunk of your profits by making purchases online and in bulk, provided you have sufficient place to store them. Bartering is trading goods and services directly with other businesses; it is a mutual exchange for the benefit of all parties that are involved. If you have an Etsy shop selling hand woven scarves and you are looking for a graphic designer who can help you design the shop poster for your Etsy shop, then all that you need to do is perhaps offer to barter with a graphic designer who resides in a region that's cold. Isn't this a win-win situation for the parties involved? You should create a master form.

When you start your Etsy business you will have to repeatedly draft emails with the same content over and over again, so instead you can create a template that you can use for answering FAQs or thanking the customers. By designing such templates you are saving on time as well as eliminating spelling errors, while seeming more professional as well.

Instead of wasting your precious time collecting the stationery that you need for shipping, you should create a shipping station. You can directly ship from your home; all you need to do is place your outgoing mail in your mailbox and it will be picked up by the postal carrier when dropping off your mail. There is also the option of online pickup as well. You should recycle your shipping supplies. Purchasing premade shipping packages as well as bubble wrap can be expensive; you can manage to save a lot of money as well as the environment by reusing your shipping supplies, provided they are still in a reusable condition. If you are opting to recycle your supplies then make sure that you mention this in your shop policies.

When determining your shipping costs, make sure to weigh your items as it is easy to lose money on shipping if you estimate the weight rather than confirming it. Shipping is an expected part of purchasing online, and customers should expect to pay those costs; you as a seller are not required to incur those costs. You can also buy postage online to save money, and sometimes you may be able to get discounts from certain shipping companies if you have an account or do bulk shipping.

If you are working from your home, then you can make use of certain tax deductions. For instance, you might be making use of a room in your own house for business purposes, use your car and even your phone line for the same reason. In this manner, you needn't have to invest separately for this purpose. You should set up short term goals that can help you work towards accomplishing something. It is easier to attain your goals when they are small and attainable. It will also provide you the necessary motivation for working harder. The last thing that you need to do is for you to get off your computer. Etsy can be very engaging, so you will need to make sure that you don't get addicted to it and squander away your precious time.

You can also save time by going mobile: you may want to consider using the "Sell on Etsy" app, which will allow you to do your work on Etsy while out and about, rather than only being able to work on your shop when you are at a computer.

Making use of the automatic renewal option for your listings is another time-saver, as it will avoid having your items expire but you won't have to do anything to renew them, or have to remember when they need to be renewed.

Listings Manager

Etsy introduced its listings manager as a tool to help sellers spend less time managing their listings, and more time marketing and selling their items. It has several functions that will help you to save time and efficiently manage your listings.

Listings Manager enables you to search all of your items — whether active or inactive, expired, or sold out. This can help to save time in many ways; for example, if you are creating new listings that are similar to previous ones, you can quickly find the old listing and copy the information, rather than having to create a new listing from scratch.

One of the most helpful uses of the Listings Manager is that you can use its 'Quick Edit' mode to alter the information of several items at once, rather than having to edit each item individually. If you are amending your shipping profile, for example, you will likely want to amend it for more than just one product, and you can do that quickly and easily with the Quick Edit function. You can also make use of filters to find the products that you want to edit, so that you do not have to edit all of your items if the changes only apply to some.

The Listings Manager also allows you to view the statistics for all of your listings at one time, so that you can get an idea of how popular items are compared to others, how quickly products are selling, etc. This is very useful for helping you to assess which products you may want to continue selling and which you may want to discontinue.

You can also quickly edit the thumbnail photos for your products through the Listings Manager. Rather than going through each item individually to edit the thumbnail, you can view the thumbnails of all of your products and adjust them by viewing them in the Listings Manager. This can save a lot of time and ensure that your products are being marketed to the best of your ability.

How to Offer Custom Items in Your Etsy Store

You can always accept requests for custom orders. For letting your buyers know that you are willing to take their ideas into consideration, you can add a Request Custom Item link in your shop's page. When the buyer clicks on this link, then Etsy will open up a private conversation between the buyer and the seller. The Request Custom link can also appear in the listing page of the products. For adding a Request custom link to your main page, you will have to click on the Your Shop link on the Etsy page. Towards the left side of the page, click on the link Options that's below the Shop Settings. The Shop Options page would open up and in this you need to enable the option Request Custom Item. Now, save the changes you have made. When you return to the main page you will notice a Request Custom Item link on the shop's main page. It is not just about accepting requests for customization of orders; you can also post about custom listings. By making use of custom listings, the buyers can ask for the customization of certain aspects of the item they want to buy and when they need the item by, providing the seller can accommodate such customizations.

If you are willing to provide for customization, then there are certain things that you can do. You can ask for upfront payment, because once an item has been personalized, it cannot be sold or used for any other purpose. Customization charges can be levied. All the items in which customization is available can be tagged in the listing as custom, personalized or made to order as well. You will need to specify the variations that can be made to the product. You will have to communicate with your buyer about the working of the process and shop's policies. You should give the buyer a time frame, so that they will know by when they can expect the delivery of their customized product. Before shipping the product, make sure that you have sent a picture of the same to the buyer.

You can also opt out of the customization option on products if there are certain items that you do not want to be customizable. Just go to edit your listing, and take off the check mark next to the 'Buyers can request customization' option.

When you take a custom order, the listing will not show up in your public shop, or in a search. However once the sale has been processed, the item will appear on your 'Sold Items' page.

If you do not want to go the full custom order route, you do have other options. You can use the variations option if there are only a couple of possible alterations, or you can note in the item's description that personalizations are available — such as engraving a name on a piece of jewelry.

Things to consider before starting an Etsy shop

Etsy is a wonderful platform for all aspiring entrepreneurs dealing in handmade crafts and arts as well as vintage items. But there are some things that you will need to take into consideration before you enter the Etsy Seller pool.

Do your research: whether it is an idea that has come to you recently, or it is something that you have been doing for a while now, you will need to do sufficient online research before creating your own E-commerce business. Listing on Etsy isn't the only criteria; you will also need willing buyers for your items. While you are researching you will need to see whether there is any demand for the items that you are making. You might consider doing a survey of potential target audience members, to see if there is interest. Are there any similar items already on sale, the price at which your competitors are selling the similar products? If you don't come across any similar products, then think of the reasons why you didn't. Research if the product you are making is viable or not, the uses your items would have for the customers and the amount of money you will need to charge them for the product you are offering along with the shipping policy. If you are able to answer these questions, then you can move ahead with your Etsy idea.

Think like a buyer: When deciding on how to describe your items, determine shipping prices, take item photos, and do other shop management, take some time to consider what you would want if you were a buyer. Imagine how you would search for a similar product, or what information you would want to see on a shop page. Take that information into consideration when setting up your shop.

Originality: Originality can be understood as a fresh take on an existing thing, its design or style. It is highly likely that the product that you are offering on sale is not the only product that is available in a specific category and you will definitely have competitors. So, in such a situation you will need to have something that would set you apart from the rest. You will need to be able to answer certain questions if you want to decide whether or not your product has some originality. The features that make your product stand out? There obviously will be some competition, so why would a customer choose your product over that of your competitor? What do you offer that your competitors don't? What makes your item unique and not like the other items already available? If you come to the conclusion that there is no product like the one that you are selling, then how will you grab your buyer's attention? Once you have done a fair share of research and know that your product has some originality, and then you will need to think about your target audience.

Target market: every business needs to have a target audience. Your target audience would be those who might be interested in buying what you have got to offer. If you don't have a clear idea about who would purchase your product, then you should probably reconsider because it is likely that no one is going to buy your product. If you are able to identify your target market, then you can take steps in the right direction to improve your sales and expand your business someday. There are some simple questions that will help you figure out your target audience. Whom do you picture as your customers, their age, sex, occupation etc.? Why would they purchase your product? How will your target customers find you, will it be online, on social media or should you consider other forms of advertisement? Will your customers want to repeat the sale that they have made?

Time is money: This is true and however cliché it might sound, it still stands true especially when you have your own business. You will need to know the amount of time that you are willing to dedicate towards your store on Etsy. If you don't have the time for creating and maintaining a store on Etsy, then you won't be successful. The successful stores on Etsy are well maintained and are being updated on a regular basis regardless of the sales that are flowing in. You will need to put in a lot of time as well as effort if you really want to make it big. You will need to make sure that your shop is updated regularly, welcoming and informative. Your advertisement and marketing strategy needs to be good and help you attract the attention of your target audience. You will need to have well drafted shipping policies, an about page and all the information that you think your customers will need. Your job doesn't end after opening up the Shop on Etsy, but you will need to actually run the shop as well. This means that you should keep checking the shop regularly, answer any questions you might get, change listings and respond to sales. Maintaining a shop on Etsy is similar to maintaining one in real life. So, you will need to keep taking care of it regularly. You will also need to promote your store and keep advertising about it for improving your sales. The more creative you are the more attention you are likely to get.

Etsy Style: There are a lot of items that people could sell at the local crafts fair or to their friends and family, products that work really well off Etsy but somehow don't work on Etsy. It is not just about doing research for your product alone, you also need to familiarize yourself with the Etsy marketplace. Have you ever purchased anything from Etsy? Take a good look around and understand this marketplace, because Etsy isn't eBay and it isn't even a local craft fair. So you will need to ensure that your product is a good fit for Etsy. You will need to research if people would be willing to buy your product, if they would be willing to choose your product over the rest, the price that they are willing to pay and if what you are doing is a hobby or are you actually interested in pursuing it as an occupation. If you are not able to answer these questions to convince yourself, then you should probably reconsider setting Shop on Etsy. If you have answers to all these questions, then you can go ahead and start making the best possible use of Etsy, because Etsy is definitely the place for you.

Etsy is a great place for selling your products, but you will need to put in a lot of time and effort, also you need to be patient because it will take a while for the results to show positively. Don't give up just because your items haven't started selling like hotcakes within a few weeks; you need to give it time for your brand to build, for people to get to know you and your products, and for your reputation as a seller to be established. Also do not set unrealistic or unattainable goals for yourself. Create small milestones that you want to reach, and work toward them. Otherwise, you will burn out, or get discouraged, before you have even given your shop and yourself the chance to succeed.

Keep updated: Letting your shop sit stagnant with the same products day in and day out will not help with marketing your shop or improving your business. Try to renew your listings or list new products, as applicable. Adding new or updated products will bring customers back to your page, whereas if your page looks the same for weeks on end then a customer is unlikely going to continue returning in the hopes that you might have introduced a new product.

Manage your finances: You may also want to consider investing in a good bookkeeping program, or hiring a bookkeeper if numbers are not your thing. Income taxes and sales taxes need to be kept properly, not only for your purposes but for legal reasons. If your shop does start to become successful, you don't want to spend all of your time trying to add up numbers when you could be concentrating on boosting your business even more.

Use the resources available to you: Etsy provides a whole variety of free resources to sellers. From policies, to help articles, to forums and teams, and several different online tools, there is help available for any problem and answers for any question that you might have. Do not hesitate to use those resources; they are there for you, and will be the support that you need as you figure out your shop and get yourself established.

Veronica McKinnon

Chapter 3
Buying and Selling

Timing your Etsy post

For making sure that the Etsy listing you are about to post reaches as many potential customers as possible you will need to plan a little. Once you have posted your listing then you can access your account at any given point of time to view your listing till it expires. When you post your listing on Etsy, within the a few seconds, the same would appear on the main page of Etsy under the tab of recently listed items. To ensure that the maximum number of buyers can see your posting, then you should consider posting it at a certain time.

If your target audience happens to be mothers on East Coast, then it would prove to be helpful if you post your listing at 9.30 EST, after they have put their young ones to sleep or 12.15 PST, when everyone in California is on a lunch break. Since Etsy is an international organization, the odds are that regardless of the time you post the listing at, it would happen to be peak time at some place or the other. If your schedule doesn't permit you to create a listing during the peak times, you needn't worry. You can create a listing in your free time and when the time is right you can just submit your listing. For doing this, instead of selecting the Publish button once you have created your listing, you should instead click the Save as Draft option. Whenever you are ready to post your listing, then you just need to go to Your Account, open the Draft Listings option that's available on the left side of the page, click on the checkbox that's present beside a listing and then click the Publish button so that you can upload your listing. Any listing that is posted on Etsy lasts for 120 days, unless the item has been sold or the listing is deactivated.

You can find out the date on which a particular listing would expire by logging into your Etsy account and then click on the currently for sale link that's there under the option Items. Now, locate the listing whose expiry date you want to know and this date appears in the expiration column besides a listing. If your Etsy shop has multiple listing, then you can sort them according to their date of expiration. For doing so, you need to click on the Expires column header on the page.

Setting up payment methods on Etsy

While payment methods were briefly discussed under the "How to set up a shop on Etsy" section, this section will talk about payment methods in more detail. There are multiple payment methods that you can choose from for your Etsy shop. However, depending upon your preferences, one or several of these options might be ideal for your Etsy business. The different methods of payment that you can opt for are as follows. Credit card is one option. During the Etsy Direct Checkout feature it can accept payment via credit cards like Visa, MasterCard, American Express and Discover. This is the most popular form of payment on the site though this feature is only available in the United States. Direct Checkout also provides Etsy users with protection that would prevent fraud and also enables you to purchase and also print U. S. Postal Service shipping labels from your Etsy shop. You will need to pay a processing fee of 3 percent of the total sale and this includes the shipping and sales tax. PayPal is a popular payment option.

All the electronic payments can be deposited within no time to your PayPal account and you can transfer money freely and easily from your PayPal account to the bank. If you are old school, then you can opt for the simple money order. For those who shy away from technology, then this is a good option. But the disadvantage of making use of this method is that the payment cannot be rendered immediately. You will have to patiently wait for the money order to arrive via snail mail. Payment via personal checks also has the same advantages and disadvantages as the ones that money order would have. There will be a delay of payment when compared to the other methods of instant payment. If you wish to, then you can accept other forms of payment such as cashier's checks or any other form of payment as you may see fit.

Once you have decided the form of payment that you want to accept, you will need to indicate the same on Etsy. Click the Your Shop link that's at the top of the Etsy page. Once this page opens, click on the Get Paid tab or Shop Payment option. If you want to select credit cards or gift cards for mode of payment, then select the Etsy's Direct Checkout option. For enabling the Direct Checkout option, you will have to click on the Sign Me Up button and the terms and conditions of this service will be displayed. Read through the terms of service carefully and then click on the Continue option to accept them. Etsy will ask you to fill out your personal information such as your name, date of birth, and the last four digits of your Social Security number or your tax ID issued by the federal government, home address, phone number and business name. You needn't worry, because this information won't be made public. It is for internal use only.

Once you have entered all this information, then you will have to click on the Continue option. The next step is to enter your bank details, the type of account, name of the account owner, bank's routing number as well as your account number. The last step is to click on the Sign Me Up option once you have filled out all the necessary information and Etsy will enroll you for Direct Checkout. If you want to accept other forms of payment like PayPal, money orders or so on, then you will need to click on the Get Paid tab and click the Additional Payments Methods option and when the list would be displayed. You will have to tick those payment options that you would want. After this you will need to save the changes. The method of payment that you have opted for is a global setting and it isn't restricted to any particular region.

Things to include in your shipping policy

Unless you want to be the seller who would knowingly want to keep his customers in the dark about how and when they could expect the delivery of their items, you will need to have a clear policy regarding shipping. When you are developing your shipping policy, there are a few things that you will have to keep in your mind.

The first thing that you will need to do is select a carrier that you want to use for shipping. It could be the U.S. Postal Service, FedEx, DHL, UPS or any of the other various available options. Once you have selected your carrier, you will need to select a specific delivery option like you can opt for First Class, Priority Mail or Media Mail as well, depending upon your requirements.

You will need to decide whether or not you want to include delivery confirmation or shipping insurance. It would be better to have shipping insurance, especially when the items you are dealing in are costly, because if at all a package gets lost in transit; you will at least be able to get your cost back. You need to decide whether or not you are willing to ship internationally.

If you are willing to ship internationally then you will need to decide if the buyer will have to incur the Customs charges. The manner in which you can handle combined shipping. Often at times, sellers offer discounts when the buyers purchase multiple items from their Etsy store in a single transaction. But it is up to you whether or not you want to follow this practice. You will also have to decide how quickly you will be able to ship the items they have purchased. There are some sellers who promise to ship the item within one day, and then there are those who will take a while longer. Whatever you have decided about the time taken for shipping, you will need to specify the same to your buyers as well. If you are taking orders for customized items, then you will have to take into consideration the time taken for customization as well. There might be a situation where the buyer needs the product as soon as possible and in such a situation you should be willing to upgrade your mode of shipping to accommodate such buyers. The last thing that you need to decide would be the manner in which you want to ship your products; you can also provide the option of gift-wrapping provided it is doable.

Etsy's Seller Protection Program

Try as hard as you want to, not every transaction will be smooth and you will definitely hit a few bumps along the way. Thankfully, Etsy offers Seller Protection. This program makes sure that your account status will remain unchanged even if a buyer reports a particular problem with your Etsy shop. There are certain things that you will need to do if you want to be eligible for the Seller Protection Program. You will need to publish all your shop policies regarding shipment, exchange of orders, returns and customization operations on the Policy page of your Etsy shop. Try and communicate with the buyers via convos instead of emails or other options. The items in your list need to have photographs that are accurate without any distortions of color; size, material and the description should give the buyer a genuine feel of what they are buying.

Make use of the tools that are offered by Etsy, provide your buyers with a date for expected shipment and make sure that their shipment reaches them on time. Ship the items to the address that is listed on the Etsy receipt or to any other address that the buyer has agreed upon. After you have shipped the items, mark the same on Etsy. If your item is priced more than

$250, then you can make use of the tracking method to confirm the signature at delivery. You should provide proof of shipping and for the items that are shipped within U.S. you need to keep a track of the proof of delivery as well. Respond to any disputes and contact the buyer who is involved in such an incident within seven days.

In addition to this, you should also respond to any queries that are sent by Etsy as well. An added bonus of this program is that it provides full coverage for items that are purchased through the Direct Checkout tool of Etsy up to a value of $1,000. So, if a good transaction goes south, then you will be in the clear. This program isn't available for all the products. For instance, transactions involving any digital goods or items that are to be delivered electronically aren't included.

Chapter 4
Successful Start on Etsy

Starting a business on Etsy might seem overwhelming. There are some things that you can do for ensuring that this process becomes more manageable and fun as well. In this chapter we will take a look at the simple steps for ensuring that you have a successful start on Etsy. With all the new concepts you need to familiarize yourself with, different strategies and terminologies that you need to learn, starting your first business on Etsy can seem like a maiden voyage to a foreign land. It can take you a while to become comfortable with your online shop and to ease this process, here are some simple guidelines that will help you out.

The first thing that you need to do is gather all the essential supplies you will need. Get all your building blocks in place so that you can go about starting your new business. This might initially take up some time but it will definitely make the process of starting and maintaining your Etsy shop easy. You can create your own checklist for ensuring that you have everything that you need. The next thing that you need to do is choose a name for your shop. You will need to opt for a name that defines the kind of items you are dealing in while also providing you with an opportunity for further expansion in the future. You wouldn't want to restrict your business ideas. For example, if you are starting off selling quilts you would not want to name your shop "Quilts Only," because in the future, should you decide to branch off and offer other products, this won't be as obvious to your potential customers with a name solely dedicated to quilts. Your shop name is going to stick by you till you deactivate a particular account, so you will need to choose the name carefully.

The goals that you are setting for yourself need to be attainable. No point in trying to set goals that are unattainable, all this will do is make you feel dejected. So, set goals that are both short term and long term. Whenever you achieve any of the goals, you need to congratulate yourself because this will act as motivation for you to achieve your long-term goals. Even if you don't achieve a particular goal, you needn't feel dejected, just remember that you will have to face a lot of obstacles and every time you have a setback don't think of it as a failure, instead think of it as a learning experience. The search option on Etsy works in a manner similar to any search engine on the web.

Potential buyers will start out by searching for a particular product by typing out some related words.

If you want to be a successful seller and want to attract all the traffic, then you should consider making use of keywords. Keywords will ensure that the potential customers are all diverted to your products and listings before other sellers. Spend sufficient time and put in some effort when you are taking the photographs of your products. This might not seem like a big deal to you, but it really is. You need to remember that the only way in which a buyer will select your product is if it appeals to them. Since it is an online platform, there is no option for physically seeing the product. The buyer will consider buying the product only when the product seems attractive. But this doesn't mean that you distort the images to provide the buyer with unrealistic expectations regarding the product. Keep experimenting with different lighting and angles till you find one that will perfectly suit your needs. Don't try to be a perfectionist. You will need to remember that a sale completed is better than you wasting your time to obtain a product that is absolutely perfect.

In your bid to obtain perfection you might forget that you have to make sales as well. The listing that you have created needs to be well curated and should make the buyer want to make a purchase. Your shop should be conducive of making a sale. Your products need to hold appeal to various shoppers and not just one particular category of shoppers. It would help if you were offering products that would fall into different price brackets. This will help in attracting more customers.

Etsy's Do's and Don'ts

There are some things that you should avoid doing on Etsy. After all, it is an online marketplace and there are certain guidelines that you should follow. Every member on Etsy should go through the DOs and DON'Ts page on the website. This page spells out in great detail the things that you can do and should not do for avoiding a potentially embarrassing incident. For viewing this page you need to click on the link that is present on the upper right corner of all the Etsy pages and click the Site Policies link and then click on the Dos and Don'ts link. Make sure that you have gone through this page to avoid breaking any site policies unknowingly. Here is a brief description of everything that is included in this page.

Membership is the section where the guidelines are given to the members regarding the manner in which they should conduct themselves on the website; it specifies whether or not ownership of an Etsy account can be transferred from one part to another, the guidelines for maintaining multiple accounts as well as the scenarios in which you can have more than one account.

Conversations, also referred to as convos, are the section that allows for the various Etsy users to communicate with one another and build healthy relationships. This is very helpful when you want to communicate about the listings and different policies of the sellers. Convos should not be used for spamming, promoting any illegal content or for harassing a fellow account user. A transaction is the section where Etsy provides clarification regarding its role in transactions and provides all the policies that are related to the transactions between both the buyers and sellers. This also indicates the steps that can be taken by the seller when the buyer defaults payment and the steps that a buyer can take when the seller doesn't hold up his end of the bargain.

If anyone on Etsy wants to give feedback regarding the performance of a buyer or a seller's goodwill, this is the section for you to do so. But there are certain guidelines that need to be followed even while providing a feedback. Marketplace criteria gives the lowdown on the kind of behavior that is acceptable and isn't on the website regarding sale and purchase. Many of the Etsy sellers would be interested in making use of different advertisement tactics for getting more publicity for their items and shops, but there are certain specifications that they need to follow and these rules are mentioned under the category Advertising on Etsy. Members on Etsy can make use of the

Flagging feature for alerting if there are any potential features with the site or they can even flag the behavior of a certain seller or buyer on the site as well.

As far as common sense goes, individuals should exhibit common sense when involving themselves in a marketplace such as this. Do not recreate previous works of art and claim they are your own without first speaking to the original artist and requesting permission. Do not start conversations with individuals if you do not intend to seek advice, product information, company information, or help. Do not price your items low to sell them easier; if you have a good, solid, creative product, then you should price it as such. Don't sell yourself short.

Advanced Marketing Strategies

Search Engine Optimization: Search Engine Optimization (SEO) is a set of strategies and techniques that will help to increase visitors to a website, by ensuring that the site places high in search results on search engines such as Google, Bing, Yahoo, and others.

Generally speaking, when a potential purchaser does an online search for an item, they are likely not going to look past the first or second page of results. So you want to make sure that your listings, or your shop, show up on the first page if possible.

In order to make the best of use SEO techniques, there are a few tips that will assist. First, remember that content is the driver for all search results: the content in your titles, item descriptions, profile picture all contribute to your shop showing up in search results.

Try to create content that is unique and accurate, so that your products are described as clearly as possible using words that will show up in search results. If you have products that are similar to each other, use descriptions that differentiate the items. For example, if you are selling wool sweaters of different colors, rather than calling them both "wool sweater with argyle pattern", you could describe one as "cream wool sweater with green argyle pattern" and "black wool sweater with blue argyle pattern." In this way, the product descriptions are both unique (cream versus black, green argyle versus blue argyle) and accurate, and use words that a potential buyer might use to find a certain product.

Links are another major factor in increasing the chances of your shop being located in search engine results. The more links to your shop online, the higher that your shop will rank in the search engine results. If you have a blog, make sure to put links to your shop and some specific listings on it, without being too excessive. If you have had your items featured on a blog or other site that belongs to someone else, ask them if they can put a link on their site to your shop; they may not agree, but it doesn't hurt to ask. On your Etsy shop, you can link between listings; these internal links will show that pages are related, which increases the rankings in the search engines.

Do NOT buy a link or use spam techniques like directory listings, as search engines can usually detect these methods, and it could also potentially irritate potential customers.

The importance of marketing on social media has been discussed in previous chapters, in terms of building your brand and getting your products out there. A presence on social media will also help to increase your shop's ranking in search engine results; the more that your shop and your products are discussed online, the more likely they are to show up in the first few results in a search.

Once you have started to implement these SEO strategies, remember that they will take time to kick in — your shop won't automatically start to increase in rankings for the search engine results.

Email marketing and eNewsletters

It may seem strange to include email marketing under advanced strategies since it has been around long before Etsy itself. But reinvigorating this 'old school' marketing technique in a way that is unique to Etsy can really help you to boost your business. Create a list of people who have bought items from you, or who have shown interest in your products before. Using this list, send these people information about your products, any sales that you are putting on, and any other relevant shop information. You should also include some fun facts or other interesting content, to make people really want to read it. You can send the information either through email or via a more formal eNewsletter.

People often focus primarily on social media for marketing, especially when it comes to online stores. But do not underestimate the value of delivering a specific readable item to previous and potential customers; in this era of online marketing, a simple email or eNewsletter just might help you stand out from the crowd.

Maintain your intellectual property

Copyright and trademark have been addressed a few times in this book, in terms of making sure that you are not infringing someone's copyright or trademark rights when you are creating product descriptions, shop names, etc. However, it is also important for you to make sure that your intellectual property (IP) rights are not being infringed. Keep an eye out for products that are too similar to yours, and that may be infringing your IP rights. If you notice that another seller has an item that is too close to yours, you should consider sending the seller a message and request to stop selling the item. If you are not sure about whether an item is something that would be close enough to yours to infringe your IP rights, then consult with an IP lawyer; this is likely a good idea before you contact another seller.

If you do have a problem with another seller infringing your IP rights, try to avoid discussing it on the forums. It may be tempting to warn other sellers about the individual, or to complain about your situation, but you do risk a claim for defamation if your comments end up damaging the seller's business and it later turns out that, pursuant to the applicable law, their product is not actually infringing.

Pop-up Markets

While the overall purpose of Etsy is to allow people to sell their products online without requiring a brick and mortar location, sometimes as a seller you just want to get out and interact with your customers. Recently, Etsy pop-up markets have taken place in different locations around North America. In Canada, for example, a specific day in September 2015 was set as a day for Etsy pop-up markets, with markets appearing in thirty-five cities across the country. This one-off day marketed the physical locations as a unique opportunity, rather than the standard brick and mortar store, which increased interest and made it seem more special to potential customers. If you are interested in participating in a pop-up market, do some research and see if there is one scheduled at a location near you. It just might be that extra little push that your Etsy store needs to get to the next level, and it can be an excellent way to meet other Etsy sellers near you and create a local team of support.

Timing your shop's rollout

Earlier in this book we talked about timing the posting of item listings to make your product more likely to be seen by potential customers and captured in search results. But the timing of your individual products is not the only timing decision that you need to make. You should also consider when you are going to officially launch your shop, especially if there is something about your shop or your products that lends itself particularly well to a certain time of year. For example, if you are selling summer footwear, then you are not likely going to find a lot of business at first if you launch your shop in November — at least for most North American customers! On the other hand, if you make Christmas decorations, then November would be an excellent time for the introduction of your business.

You can conduct some basic research to find out when your type of product sells best; the information is not guaranteed to be out there, especially if you have a niche type of product, but it doesn't hurt to look. You just might find some information that will be very helpful for deciding when to open your Etsy shop.

Use Pinterest to its full advantage

Pinterest is a social media platform that works a little differently than Facebook and Twitter. Unlike the other social media sites, your focus with Pinterest is not to create a page for your business, but to encourage Pinterest users to 'pin' your products to their Pinterest board. The products in your Etsy shop will automatically have a "Pin It" button (the same goes for sharing to Facebook, Twitter, and other social medial platforms), so it is easy for people to pin your products to their board.

Having your products linked on someone Pinterest board helps in two main ways. First, it will improve your shop's or product's search ranking results, when it comes to search engine optimization. Second, many Pinterest users will browse other Pinterest users' boards to get ideas, and if your products are pinned, then that increases your shop's exposure and encourages online visitors to your store.

In order to use Pinterest to the fullest extent, however, you need to work with its analytics function. To do this, you will need to have a Pinterest account, so that you can enable the analytics for your Etsy shop or related website. Once you have enabled the analytics in your Pinterest account, you have to get your Meta Tag (a line of computer code specific to your account).

Once you have the Meta Tag, you will need to paste the Meta Tag into your other social media platforms — your blog or website, Tumblr, etc. This involves editing the coding for your sites (which is why you cannot do it for Twitter or Facebook, as you are not allowed to edit that code for your individual account), so you may want to recruit someone with computer programming knowledge to assist you.

Once you have installed the Meta Tag wherever you are going to install it, you can then go back to your Pinterest account and view the analytics, which will show how many 'pins' have been made from each of your sites. Not only will it show the pins directly from your site to a Pinterest board, but it will also show you how often those pins have been shared with other Pinterest users. In addition to that information, you can also find out how often people clicked on a pin and went to your website, and which are your most shared or clicked products. All of this information is extremely useful for assessing how your marketing strategies are working, which products are most popular online, and which products just are not getting enough interest to make it worth it to continue their production.

Pinterest analytics is a bit of a complicated concept, and you may need some outside help to use it properly. But considering how useful the information is that you can obtain from this analytics function, it is well worth the time and effort that you might put in to use it properly.

Chapter 5
Growing Your Base

The previously mentioned techniques will help you get a strong starting base. They'll be all you need in order to get started with your shop and creating a little chatter for your products. However, in the long term, you need to know the ins and outs of the resources you have at your disposal. It's not enough to create a newsletter, for example. You need those newsletters to turn into sales, and there are techniques to help you with just that. All in all, you need to channel your inner social media guru in order to keep your shop in everyone's eyes and ears.

In this chapter, we'll explore everything related to Search Engine Optimization—in terms of Etsy and blogging. You'll be equipped with the latest techniques and tools which can help you on your selling journey. Next, we'll take a little time to really explore each social media channel. Lastly, to wrap everything up, we'll discuss some example shops from different categories and check how we can use everything we've learned so far in practical settings.

SEO and Etsy

We've already discussed the ABCs of SEO, so let's take a look at more advanced stuff. Feel free to jump on over to the previous chapter if you've forgotten what SEO is.

As previously mentioned, search engines use keywords in order to display related posts during a search. While there is more to SEO than just keywords, Etsy does most of the job for you. Being an established website which wants to earn through its sellers and buyers, Etsy already optimizes its platform to appear in a search engine; you simply need to use the proper keywords and meet the web site halfway. As you might have guessed, you need to use words which are being searched by other users on the internet. But how do you find what's trending on the internet these days?

We live in a fickle time. Trends change really fast, and most shops need to keep up with the times in other to generate a lot of hype for their products. If nothing else, sometimes a word can make all the difference in the world. So knowing what attracts your potential buyers or what words catch their eye is quite important. You can play the guessing game and conduct research by viewing what your competitors are doing, but that isn't a sure-fire way to gain sales or attract potential buyers. You could land a few buyers, but you won't be optimizing your shop to reach a wider audience. Thankfully, the internet has a bunch of tools to help you along the way. Let's take a look at some of these keyword research tools you can check out.

SEMrush

If you're looking to study competitors, SEMrush can be your best friend. Using a provided URL, you can easily get the best keywords used by your competitors in their content. Its advanced filtering system is a wonderful tool for sellers, especially if you run a blog. It goes as far as to display Cost Per Click; how much money bloggers or businesses spent into that particular keyword. The higher CPC a keyword has, the more widely it provides a return on its investment and the more attractive it is to use. SEMrush is powerful but more suited for sellers who intend to run blogs as well since there is a cost to using this service.

Google Keyword Planner

This old, but gold tool has been around for ages and was one of the first keyword optimization tools—not to mention; it's still one of the best in the market. Unlike SEMrush, you can't evaluate what keywords your competitors are using; but you can get a wider idea of which keywords are trending and which aren't. Best of all? It's a free tool anyone can use to optimize their content. All you need to do is enter a keyword you think might generate some chatter, and it'll tell you whether it will and provide you with a list of keywords ranging from highly ranked to lowly ranked.

Longtail Pro

If you have a little cash to dole up, Longtail Pro is also an excellent option. It's not only a powerful tool that operates like SEMrush and provides keywords like Google Keyword Planner, it actually adds fun to the entire research process. With a modern, intuitive design, this research tool is made for those new to SEO, but powerful enough for the pros to use. That said, it also comes with a pretty price tag which isn't quite necessary for a simple Etsy seller.

Keyword Tool.io

Want to keep things simple? Keyword Tool.io is made for just that. Using Google's Autocomplete function, this simple tool is really helpful in finding just the right keywords you can use for your website. As you search in Google, you might've noticed how it tries to guess what you're trying to search and lists a bunch of related searched using the words you've put in. This tool uses this awesome feature to provide you with a list of 750+ keywords which would all be related to your keyword. Not to mention, this is a free tool. If you're looking to get started, this tool is definitely worth checking out.

Buzzsumo

Want to sell products according to the latest internet trend? Perhaps you're dealing with some fandom works and want to stay in the know with the latest happenings. Buzzsumo is the perfect tool for that. Instead of providing you data of keywords being used, this tool provides you with what articles or posts are being shared on what platform the most. This would help you curate your posts for social media and help you understand what words you should use for each of your audiences. While this tool does display everything from Pinterest to Facebook, Instagram analytics aren't really shown on this website which might be an issue for some. Alternatively, you can even use Google Trends to see what's trending in each country and location you might want to sell your products in.

What kind of keyword should you select?

When looking for products, users will use three types of searches:

- Broad

- Phrase

- Exact

A broad keyword search will usually entail one single keyword or a bunch of unspecific keywords grouped together. Say a buyer is looking for rings to buy, they might just search *"rings etsy."* A phrase searcher will be more specific and might search along the lines of *"vintage rings, etsy"*. Lastly, an exact searcher will know exactly what they want and search for their exact word—i.e. *"black vintage rings, etsy."* Each type of searcher can be a potential buyer, so you need to cater to all three types. There is, however, a downside. The more specific your search, the lower audience you'll find; since you're basically targeting a niche. As a seller, you can counter this by catering to different types of people or using phrases, instead of exact words. That depends on what you're trying to sell and who you're trying to reach. Looking into what your competitors, on Etsy or otherwise, are doing is a good policy when it comes to this. You need to find a keyword which balances between high search ability and good traffic. The better your SEO ranking, the more exact you can get.

How and where should keywords be used?

The first thing to always remember is: Don't litter your text with your keyword. Many people love Etsy for its personal feel; everything from the handmade products to the messages is personalized and don't feel robotic. You can find your own perfect technique, but here are a few guidelines which work for most people:

- **Use multiple keywords:** Don't restrict yourself to one keyword per listing. You need to have one main keyword, but it's generally healthy to keep 3-4 keywords, depending on your product description.

- **Vary your keywords depending on different search types:** Use some which are for broad searches, while others for those who use exact keywords. This will help you cater to each type.

- **Use your main keyword in your heading/title:** Now you might see quite a few keywords being used in Etsy heading. You'll have gift baskets titled "Gifts for her + Bridal shower gift + Bridesmaid's gift" and those work well enough to cater to different types since they all target different audience, but if you have only one audience, simply use one simple keyword in your title to make sure your audience is able to find your product.

- **Use keywords in your product description naturally:** As discussed, having a voice in your content is important. As a general rule, you should mention your keyword around 1% times in your content. Say, you have a description of 300 words, use your keyword only 3 times within the text. If you're using multiple keywords, it's great if you can use each keyword the same way, but not a necessity. You can lower the count of your secondary keywords, especially if your secondary keywords are present in your main one. Additionally, it's generally good to include your first main keyword in the few 1-2 lines of your content, so search engines immediately identify your keyword as being related to a particular keyword's search.

Just by using these tips, you'll be able to see massive differences in your shop's visibility and ranking. That said, Etsy does most of the job for you when it comes to SEO rankings. If you're starting your own blog, you need to understand a few more things about optimization in order to make your blog into an asset for your online business.

SEO and blogging

When you create a website, it's like a newborn baby on the internet. Precious to you and full of possibilities, but it's just another kid in the world wide web. It needs a little help and polish before people start noticing it and even more effort to help it become a fully functioning website. Luckily, search engine optimization techniques are present to be your parenting guide in this scenario.

Now we've discussed in detail how keyword research can be used to optimize your content, but the content is one simple (yet important) part of it. That said, there are more important parts which on a platform like Etsy, you don't need to worry about; but on your own blog, you definitely have to.

Why have a blog anyway?

You might wonder why bother developing taking up this headache then. For one, blogs are able to do what Etsy isn't: Develop your individual brand. Now you can become a brand through Etsy, but you'll still be another Etsy seller, only reaching the crowd that visits the site. That is great for a while, given the website is visited by millions from all over the world; but you need to gain more potential buyers faster and wouldn't it feel good to bring in buyers through your talents? A blog would also give you a following, securing yourself a nice niche to work out from. You can have a community which can guide you in what they want by commenting and emailing you, so you can really connect with your buyers.

How to get started?

It all starts with your website. For a good SEO score, the first and foremost thing you need is a website. Your domain name should be from your website: Short, easy to remember and something which defines you. In most cases, you'd want to your store name to match your website name, but it's not necessary. As long as your blog is able to direct traffic to your store, it's all good.

The second thing to ensure is your website's code. Now you can set your own blog using content management systems (such as Wordpress, Blogspot, or Joomla) or get a specialized website made by a designer. Each method can work, but you need to ensure your website's code is efficient. Web sites which are heavy with unnecessary code load slower can have lots of bugs and won't get you the eyeballs you need. The better the code, the easier it makes for search engines to load up your website and rank it better. There are a bunch of tools available to check how efficient your website is, but we recommend checking out QuickSprouts or Moz.com for more rounded results. Note: If your blog is fairly new, some aspects will not be as efficient since your blog doesn't have much content on it. You can use these tools to fix any problems you can or continually stay on top before any problem can arise.

This should be your starting base. Now we'll need to look at more every day on-page and off page SEO techniques. We've mentioned most of these before, but to provide you a checklist, let's list common techniques for both types.

On-page SEO includes:

- Title Tags

- H1 Tags

- Description

- Keyword Density

- Keyword Placement

Off-page SEO includes:

- Social Media

- Link Building

- Articles/Blogs

- Forum Posts

We've discussed On-Page SEO techniques in quite some detail above. Most of the same techniques you'll use for your Etsy shop will apply for your blog as well. However, there's one thing important for any seller to keep in mind when developing a blog: Pictures are worth a thousand words.

If your blog post is accompanied by an eye-catching image, you'll be able to attract 3 times more people. On Etsy, you need to show your product in a way which attracts, yet informs users of what your product is. On a blog, your main focus is presentation. If you're making a professional DIY website to accompany your own handmade items, your DIY projects need to have an attractive presentation that makes potential buyers crave those products. You should be good to do for optimizing using on-page techniques. Now, while we'll discuss social media in more detail later, discussing other off-page techniques is quite important as well. So let's dive right into it.

Off-Page SEO techniques

First off, let's start with link building. Now even if you don't have a personal blog, you can use link building to your advantage. If you have one, you prepare your website acts like a link to your Etsy shop. But as mentioned, you need quality links in order to rank higher in any search engine. You can do this through guest posts.

Now as we've mentioned, guest post is when a blog invites an individual to write in their blog—i.e. provide their readers with information, while providing you with free marketing. In many cases, the host blogger will allow you to link your products, your website or shop. You might think *great; how do I get an invitation?* Established bloggers usually do get invites to guest blog; but if you're starting out, all you need to do is ask.

While not all bloggers will jump up with enthusiasm, especially if you're a new seller. Some might be convinced by providing when with informative and eye-catching content. Now before you send anyone an article to post, research their website and their audience. Come up with an idea which helps their website rank well and interests both current and potential readers. Pitch the idea —as well as why it would be profitable to use guest blogging - to the blogger and only write your article once confirmation has been reached. Many bloggers are excited by guest posts since it helps their blog grow. If you have your own blog, they might be more inclined to provide you with a guest blog opportunity because it can help them grow as well.

Now some individuals might run private blogs, not really open for guests to blog on, but they might fit your exact niche. So what to do? For one, you can exchange your product for a review on their website. Many PR companies even for high-end brands, especially in the cosmetics sector, send out products for free to bloggers and vloggers to try out and review if they like them. You can use much the same tactic to score some traffic for your shop. You can start out by finding bloggers or vloggers who fit your niche and then contact them about how you would love to send them some items you've created. Show them some fan love and check their response. If they're open to the idea, ship your products to them. Now, you should also remember bloggers have to maintain integrity towards their readers. Many bloggers give honest reviews or only feature products they like, so try to research on what their personal likes are and personalize your gift as much as you can. Also don't hold your hopes on one blogger alone. It's their discretion whether they want to show off your products or not. The best way is to invest a little and send your free gifts to a number of different bloggers. However, this is a superb way to get some fast traffic using a reliable and authentic source in both the search engine's eyes and your potential buyers'.

Likewise, you can use different niche related forums to advertise or talk about your products and even get some feedback. The more talk you generate; the more traffic you get. Now that you have everything managed on your shop or blog end let's dive into the ever vast and ever useful world of social media.

Veronica McKinnon

Chapter 6
Becoming a Social Media Guru

Throughout this book, we've talked about social media and its importance quite by a bit. It's a facility we're blessed to have—if we know how to use it. Too often bloggers and sellers will just make their social media to never use it. A smart seller would seize the opportunity and sell his or her products through everything he or she can. That said, social media websites are quite different—not to mention, they're a dime a dozen now. The reigning champions, however, have been consistently growing in the past few years, and if you want to start anywhere, it's on them. We're talking about Facebook, Twitter, Instagram, YouTube and Pinterest. These quads will help your shop get limitless traction. We're going to look at what each one has to offer and the techniques you can use to grab on to as many potential buyers as you can from each avenue.

As we've already discussed Pinterest, we're going to do ahead and skip that. You can travel back to chapter 4 and read up on it if you need a refresher course.

Facebook

With over 1 billion people active on Facebook each month and each user spending an average of 40 minutes on the website, you sure have a lot of reach with it. Facebook is meant to be for all types of people—from your 5-year-old son to your grandmother. It is also designed to be simple, yet intuitive. And best of all: It provides ample ways to sell your Etsy products.

How to sell through Facebook?

There are a couple of ways to go about this.

First, if you're operating a simple Etsy shop. You can simply post your products with appropriate, eye-catching descriptions to get some public love. If, however, you have a website, you can mix in your blog posts and products for some soft selling.

Secondly, you can use Facebook Ads function. One of the best features Facebook provides sellers is the ability to develop their own advertisements and their own flexible campaigns. If you're simply starting out and are low on cash, a simple page which attracts traffic is certainly enough. If you have some money to invest, using ads is definitely the way to go.

How to develop effective Facebook ads to get traffic?

Facebook ads is a whole subject which deserves to be talked in much detail for you to understand how to use it. Like with anything, simple usage won't get you very far if you don't understand it. So let's first discuss what Facebook ads have to offer.

Facebook ads give you the opportunity to reach its wide audience or a part of it. You get to decide who you want to show your adverts to by selecting a niche. Individuals who've liked similar products or websites will be shown your ads. Your advert can be for your Facebook page, your blog or your Etsy shop. And perhaps the most attractive thing about Facebook, you set your own budget. Unlike advertising in traditional media or other online websites, you can make a flexible budget and really target the audience you want.

There are cons to this, however. Facebook likes, shares or even traffic does not necessarily mean you're going to sell products. People can like a post without it transferring into a sale. You'll need to really brush up on your marketing skills in order to make effective advertising campaigns on Facebook.

How to market using Facebook advertising?

Step 1: Pick your audience.

Be as specific as you can, right down to the gender and age you think your products appeal most to or the ones most likely to buy. You can even choose which geographical location you want to target.

Step 2: Align your audience and your campaign

Think about what your audience would like to see and what attracts them to such products. Facebook lets you add a personalized blurb and image to your advertisements, so you really need to make the most of it. There are many ways you can use a campaign, but a good starting method is to place a product as your image and announce a discount. Other ways you can attract users to your page or blog by promoting posts and using an image which shows your general theme. Don't forget to employ the use of a keyword in the blurb. While Facebook ads aren't listed on search engines, keywords are words being searched by people. Using them reminds them of the product they want and are more likely to get attracted.

Step 3: Test placement for your ad

Facebook allows you to place your ad in the widget area on the right, under the heading of sponsored links, or in between posts. In a mobile version, only in-post ads are available. You can choose where your ads are displayed on the website. You can select both together, depending on your budget and where you believe buyers would be able to see your ad from.

Step 4: Set a budget and hit okay

Facebook will display an average number of views or likes you'll get within your entered budget per day. While this number isn't exactly accurate; if your marketing techniques are on point, you'll be able to achieve more than the average they show.

The rest depends on your marketing skills. But don't worry, we'll be taking a look at different marketing techniques you can employ for Facebook or otherwise. Also, always remember to research your target audience and check how they reacted to your marketing campaign. It might take a few tries to get things right, but soon you'll be able to see what an asset Facebook can be for selling on Etsy.

Twitter

With around 330 million active monthly users, Twitter is also an Etsy-ian's best friend. For one, it's pretty simple to use. For another, it helps Etsy users interact in a familiar, personal tone. Facebook, for example, is a more formal affair. It can be used to conduct one to one interactions, but it doesn't breed the activity like Twitter does.

How to use Twitter to your advantage?

You need to start at the beginning and develop your account. Give it a personal, friendly feel using your description, but feel free to provide a link to your shop. Next, all you need to do is tweet. Interact with people and mingle in conversations. Somebody tweeted about needing just what you're providing? Send a tweet and get in touch with them. You can really engage people through Twitter and instead of having to hard sell, you can really soft sell your products or shop. Building relationships with like-minded people is a helpful way to grow your connections and your business. You're not just interacting with people who like the same things as you, but you might like to buy the same things. Not to mention you're giving it all a friendly touch. You can have a feedback loop with buyers who can help you sell through their word of mouth, or in this case, word of fingers.

If you're not on the corporate side and want to have a little fun as you sell, Twitter is your short and sweet way to connect with your audience. That said, hard selling on twitter might be a little difficult, and it doesn't provide Facebook easy scroll option whereby people can like and share your posts with ease. You will, however, gain traction through retweets which can really help if it's by someone who has a lot of followers. The key to Twitter? Have a brand personality.

Instagram

With around the same statistics as Twitter, the picture power of Pinterest and word power of Facebook, Instagram is an often overlooked resource when it comes to selling; but a mighty effective one.

How to use Instagram effectively?

There are two ways you can use Instagram: Use your own Instagram account to attract traffic or use Instagram influencers to do so. Instagram influencers are established Instagrammers who have a large following. Much like sending gifts, you can contact these influencers to help out if they like your product. We suggest using both. Instagram is increasing being used to carry out advertising campaigns. Although there is no advertising system in place, you can make images to call people to your store or use them to show various promotional activities. It all depends on how you choose to use this wonderful, flexible resource. Visual imagery is all that matters in Instagram, and if you need a little help determining what kind your Instagram's feed with look like with certain pictures grouped in its layout, you can use Instagram Layout app to get an exact idea of how your Insta-collage would look like to users.

While both Pinterest and Instagram are photo-related websites, the commonly shared images vary differently. And you should curate your pictures according to Instagram's normal trends if you wish to use it effectively.

YouTube

Last, but not least: YouTube. As an online product seller, you might not believe YouTube has anything to offer for you. Except you'd be entirely mistaken. YouTube is a highly recommended way to sell your products. You don't need to make infomercials to sell. Instead, you can focus on different aspects. Say, you sell hand painted works on Etsy. You can record yourself making a few viral-worthy videos by painting things YouTubers would like or give beginner's classes to those new to painting. Or you could even use YouTube as your own Vlog. Making a video blog is much like a blog, but more visual. You're getting in more personalized content, and a video adds authenticity to your work which definitely helps in selling. Not to mention, YouTube has an ads program as well which bloggers can take advantage of. You're also automatically being recommended when people watch other similar YouTubers. The more entertaining and creative you are with YouTube, the easier it will be to gain more traffic for your store.

In most cases you'll be using two or more social media channels to promote your Etsy store. In that case, you can run cross-platform campaigns, but we'll discuss more of that in the upcoming chapters. One of the best ways to gain traffic and buyers through social media on Etsy is by connecting with people and getting to know them. So don't be shy to contact different individuals; most people are friendlier than they seem and do help out—especially when they see how talented and dedicated a seller is.

That said, networking through social media isn't enough. Your work isn't simply to make your brand known among buyers, but entice them to actually make a purchase. Social networking gets you eyeballs, content and visuals get you those buy clicks. So if you're ready to explore that, just head on over to the next chapter.

Chapter 7
Getting sales

Many new or even old birds discover using social media or other small tricks aren't enough when it comes to getting those sales. You might have high enough traffic to your products, but those seeds don't seem to be giving any fruit. Sales require a little more.

Traffic means people are interested in your product, but something isn't selling on purchasing it just yet. It could be content, visuals or just lack of encouragement. Since we're looking to make you into a savvy seller, we're going to discuss these aspects in terms of Etsy, blogging, and social media. Each works in a different way, and each audience has different selling points, so it's important to know the distinction. Let's start with Etsy.

Images

Etsy

Unlike blogging, Etsy provides you with a few customizable options. The clean, attractive layout does half of the job for you. But it does the same thing for your competitors. You still need to find ways to make yourself shine. Make your Etsy store as personalized as you want, but keep the following in mind.

Images are king.

First, let's dispel the notion that you need an expensive camera to take fabulous product photos. In this day and age, you can use your handy dandy phone camera to take pictures. You just need to make sure you're doing it right.

Smartphone photography requires you to be smart and employ the tricks you have at your disposal. Studio pictures look amazing partly because of their lighting. So first off, make sure you have plenty of light. Your smartphone isn't able to produce studio-quality images in low-light and might actually result in a pretty noisy and grainy looking image. Using such images won't get you sales and might turn off potential buyers. Your image needs to show your product off to Etsy customers. So avoid taking low-quality images by shifting to a shooting area with lots of light. You can shoot near a window or even outside. You can use lamps or bulbs, but make sure they give off natural looking light.

Secondly, if you don't have a set background for your image, attach white paper to cardboard. This white background will help you and your potential buyers to really focus on your product, rather than have an image with tons of background items which might be distracting. Not to mention, a white background gives off a clean look and works really well in capturing attention.

Next, don't use your hands when taking pictures. We all tend to shake our hands when we take pictures with a camera. Your phone is, even more lightweight and small than ordinary cameras, so shakes and blurs are pretty common. Preferably you should use a tripod and maybe take a timed photo. If that's not an option, you can use a Stringpod. It's a nifty DIY tripod for stabilizing your camera in place. Take a thick string, loop it from one end and place the loop between your feet. Tie the other end to your camera and viola. You'll have a more stable picture. If, however, this isn't an option or a stringpod will not work with your smartphone, all you need to do is breathe. Our heartbeats cause our bodies to move around. So brace yourself by taking a few deep breaths before you snap that image.

Lastly, avoid zooming. It's tempting to use your phone's inbuilt zoom feature to keep close up images. Avoid the cropping step and all. But zooming is actually detrimental. It decreases the quality of your photo since you're basically enlarging it without changing the photo resolution in any way. If you really need close up images, use lenses instead. You can find a variety of photo lenses specifically made to achieve the look you're after. Marco lenses, for example, are able to take incredibly zoomed pictures. You also have the option of wide-angle, fisheye and telephoto.

Taking pictures isn't everything, though. Those images you've wowed at were probably a result of photo editing. You're not distorting, changing or falsifying your product. Instead, you simply need to enhance it so your image looks good. To have the perfect sellable image, you need to engage in a little photo editing. And it all starts with your picture taking process. Start by taking lots of images in different areas, angles, backgrounds, and placing. Having more options means you can really pick and which ones you want to use. Different images are also important for having a good portfolio for your items. One image from one angle isn't enough to satisfy customers and encourage them into hitting that buy button. On Etsy, you'll see a bunch of different types of images in top selling product listings. They usually are of four types:

The professional, studio image

This is the image we've talked about creating so far. It's your classic plain white background, well-lit and product focused image. It's the clearest way to show your product's potential to customers and help them see exactly what you're offering. Buyers are drawn toward clean, clear and bright photos, which quickly transfer information on what the product is. This is your first glance sell. It's also a realistic depiction of what the customer should expect and gives you more credibility and improves your repute. Keep in mind that lighting is very important for such pictures.

The close up

Your main image shows off your entire product, but it's time to take a dive into your customer's mind. When it comes to online retail, consumers are still skeptical about what they're getting. Is the quality up to the mark? Are there any fine details which I might not like? This is where a macro shot comes in. This fine-detail shot accentuates your product's quality and texture. For example, if you're selling a painting, having a macro shot detail of your strokes will help customers be aware of the quality they are paying for. It's preferable to have at least 2 close up shots, so you're able to give fine details of all sides.

The Full-size image

Now it's time to show your potential customers how their product looks—whether on people or things. Most commonly used in jewelry or clothing items, this shot is actually a must-have for all product listings. Why? Buyers want to know how their purchase would look in a real life setting, and this shot is meant to do just that. So, for example, you're selling a necklace; you can get a model to wear it in your image. Or, say, you're selling a wooden carved box; place it in a neat location surrounded by items a box like that traditionally would be placed. This realistic imagery will help buyers get a sense of how your product scales and the exact way they can use it.

Lifestyle Image

If you want to ensure your customers are reeled in, using a lifestyle image is quite important. This is where you make your product shine. You need to place your product in a place and surrounded by items which would make anyone crave it. You want them to imagine owning your product. Consider this an image in an advertisement. Make it fun, cute, and eye-catching.

Once you have various angles and taken plenty of them, select the bunch you like. Don't worry about shortlisting too much. You just need to narrow them down to manageable amounts. The short-listed images should be sharpened. You can use different apps on your smartphone or just use Photoshop. iOS and Android apps are more user-friendly for some individuals, so you might want to check these options out—even if to save a little time and money. You can also enhance your image's color to make colors more vivid and feel more alive. The Etsy app is able to help you with that. It includes a bunch of photo editing tools, so you don't even need to use a third-party app to achieve your goal. Using this app, you can auto-enhance your image and get a boost in brightness and color—with just one click. It also comes with several filters, including black and white, color, brightness and tilt shift. This will help you get those small adjustments your images need to make those big sales. Lastly, don't forget that crop. If your image is leaning a certain way (that doesn't look good), feel free to rotate it. Cropping the picture would help to get the composition just right. If you're unable to get the right crop, you're better off re-shooting your product. After all, you really need to get images right if you want to sell on Etsy.

Blogging

Unless you're showing off your pre-made Etsy items, you need to make images set up on your blog a little different. There needs to be more lifestyle and full-size images. If you're making DIY posts, you should include a bunch of close ups, so readers are able to pick up information quickly. It's generally good for DIY blog posts to have at least 5 images for good measure.

Social Media Images

Now with social media, you're back to feeling a little restricted in terms of layout. You can't change things to make your content look good, but need images to attract in order to sell.

First things first: Image sizes. What many people get wrong is not curating images according to each social image sizes. By getting the dimensions right, you'll be able to make proportional images which attract. Wonky pictures don't impress, even if you have an awesome product. So let's look at common social medias and their preferred image size:

- Facebook – Cover Photo: 851 x 315 px, Profile image: 180 x 180 px, Shared Images: 1200 x 630 px, Shared link: 1200 x 627 and Highlighted Image: 1200 x 717 px.

- YouTube – Channel Cover Photo: 2560 x 1440 px and Video Uploads: 1280 x 760 px.

- Instagram – Profile Image: 110 x 110 px, Photo thumbnails: 161 x 161 px and Photo size: 180 x 180 px.

- Twitter – Header Photo: 1500 x 500 px, Profile Photo: 400 x 400 px and In-Stream Photo: 440 x 220 px.

- Pinterest – Profile Image: 165 x 165 px, Board Display: 222 x 150 px and Pin Size: 236 px

- Tumblr – Profile Image: 128 x 128 px and Image Post: 500 x 750 px

- Google+ - Profile Image: 250 x 250 px, Cover image: 1080 x 608 px, Shared Image: 150 x 150 px and Shared Image: 497 x 373 px.

These image sizes should also give you an idea of where your images can be used. In addition to these, remember Facebook allows you to post ads with images so you can optimize your images accordingly.

According to some studies, photo on Facebook generates around 53% more likes than an average post. Unlike, say with blogs and even your Etsy page, you need to showing is more important than telling. If your image is able to say everything you need, you've got an effective image. You might realize, you might not always have to use product photography in social media posts. Say, you're running a discount campaign. Instead of adding a text in the description, either build a single banner announcing the discount or post images of your discounted products with the discounts clearly visible or do both.

Content

Etsy

Now that's you've caught your potential buyer's immediate attention; it's time to go in for the kill. What you write on your Etsy page matters a lot. It might make a difference between whether you actually get a purchase or not. Here are a few guidelines which might help:

- **Write important information first** – Tell potential buyers what the product is and what they're getting in the first paragraph. People nowadays want quick information and giving them that is how you reel them in. Telling them, this is exactly what they're looking for should be your starting point. This not only captures their attention but enables you to subtly drop your selected SEO keyword and improve your shop's optimization.

- **Make it about the customer** – Avoid using the word "I". Your item listing should be about your customer and the product they'll receive. Not only does this give off a bad impression, it unnecessarily lengthens your product's description. Instead, talk about your product and focus on the utility or charm it has for customers.

- **Make it visual** – Taking a cue from Etsy and the photography you'll use, keep things simple and chic. People aren't here to read articles with lumps of long paragraphs but do need some product information do understand what they're getting. So make things appealing by formatting your text properly. Etsy gives you a pretty clean font and font size to work with. Now you simply need to make sure you have small, bite-sized paragraphs and use a bullet or numbered points where necessary. As a general rule, use bullet points when your list does not need to be done in any order, and use numbered points when you're discussing a step by step process.

- **Be yourself** – But your professional self. You can have a fun or even comical tone but remain within a seller's professional word usage. Your brand needs to have personality in order to make an impression. Not to mention, personality adds authenticity to your words. It makes you seem like a true crafter proud of their work, rather than someone selling for the sake of it. You don't need to be loud with that personality, but just be yourself. If for example, you're not a Native English speaker, you can hire a translator or proofreader. If you're concerned about your translation, feel free to add that you've used one.

- **Be clear about what you're selling** – Part of anyone's objection against online shopping is misinformation about what they purchase. For example, you could display your products in a basket, but unless you state the basket is included, customers won't know. When you're going through such efforts to package your products in a clear and appealing way, don't let your writing be the shortfall. Also, inform the customers of how much they are getting. You can place 2 or 3 versions of items in your product images, but stating you sell each one separately or whether it's a pack. Additionally, adding the dimensions of your products is always a good policy. The more information you give, the more informed your customers feel. This gives a good impression, makes them feel confident in their purchases and helps to avoid confusion where you can.

- **Leave with a conversation starter** – Encourage your customers to contact you if they have any questions. It starts a conversation with them and encourages them to do so. This works especially well for products where personalization is important as your potential customers are able to see your friendly, open personality and are more likely so contact you. So be accessible as much as you can.

- **End with more promotion** – Many times customers might stumble upon one of your links, but be interested in other, similar products. Even if it's just a different variation of the product. If you do nothing, customers will leave or bounce away without noticing you have exactly what they need. That's not really efficient for you. So when you're ending your description, add a few hyperlinked links to similar products potential customers might be interested in. Additionally, you can add your social media or website in order to tie everything together and generate positive links (remember the concept of back linking we talked about a few chapters ago?). Add authenticity, professionalism and good selling techniques to grab all the customers you can using your product's listing details.

Website/Blog

Blogging and websites will contain different information from your Etsy store. You can include listing, but it would be better not to defuse your customers like that. If you go to a DIY tutorial website, content preferably is informative, yet minimal. You can add words to add your personality and give a personalized feel, but instructions should be clear cut. Using standardized formats and even measures is a good way of staying consistently tidy with your content. How you sell your Etsy page can be through adding a "You can also purchase this at my shop" at the end of the page for individuals who love your product, but aren't inclined to undergo a DIY project.

Alternatively, you can link, mention and show images of your more polished Etsy products and use them as examples for your current DIY post. You don't really sell your product, but indirectly mention it in a way which excites others about it.

Lastly, you can have blog posts about your featured Etsy items per week or month in blog posts to share things you've created and talk about how excited you are or what you were hoping customers get from using your product in such a situation.

In ads, however, you can do more. Placing a pop-up ad on your website with a coupon code for your Etsy store (in exchange of their emails) is a great way to increase your mailing list, encourage people to check out your store, and make a purchase. Since it's your blog and free space for yourself, you can be as creative as you like with how you choose to sell.

Social Media

As we've discussed, social media needs to be a visual experience as much as possible. It's about engagement and giving potential customers a push in the direction they're clearly interested in. Etsy, being an online handicraft store, is for individuals who love personalized items. That holds true when it comes to social media as well. These are people who appreciate hard work and love seeing original, creative works. Use that as your cue in order to break through social media and capture their interest.

When it comes to Facebook, use it to tell your brand's story. Twitter for connection. Pinterest and Instagram for showing off your talent. Each one of these social media platforms helps to improve engagement in a way which aids in a sales boost. Run campaign and adverts through them, and make sure of proper words.

And what are proper words?

Proper words, or should we say buzz words, are easily identifiable words which catch a reader's eye and some which nudge them in the direction you want. These words may include something as simple as 'get' or even 'you'. They're the ones that make a difference. Which allow you spread your story and your brand name with ease. Make people want to buy, if you will.

Let's take a look at some words you can use to really sell your product in subtle ways:

- You – Make your customer a part of the conversation. Make them feel like you're invested solving their problem—even if it's just buying a chic new ring to wear at parties or being unable to decide what to gift their bridesmaids. Use you as early as possible in your text and make sure to replace it wherever you've used 'I', if you can.

- Can – This tells customers you're able to do something for them or that they can do something with your product. Giving off a can-do attitude in terms of selling and what you're selling can be a huge change.

- Easy – Nobody really likes putting in an effort if they don't have to, and easily conveys them just that. Telling customers that you or your product can make their life easy in any way is something most people become heavily intrigued by.

- Get – Like easy; it gives customers a stake on hearing you out. They're getting something from purchasing your product. There are tons of material items in the world, but your product gets them the utility they want.

- New – New items are always alluring. It's a mystery you want to discover. This word can some exceptionally handy when it comes to social media.

- Exclusive – Etsy lets you list a few exclusive, limited edition items by setting for how long an item should be available for buyers. Crafty items which are exclusive or in limited amounts usually are able to lay seed to this 'get it while it's hot' mentality within potential buyers.

- Exciting – In many cases, buyers feel exactly what you write. If you say your product is mediocre, they'll view it as that. But who would want to say that if they wish to sell their crafted works? Instead, use excited to pump potentials into exploring more. I

- Free – Who wouldn't love something free? Now you might be wondering: But why would I want to give something for free when I want to earn. When it comes to selling, you don't need to give high priced items for free. Free can be something as simple as a gift box. The word free itself gives a positive impression more than the actual item.

- Gift – Same case with a gift. At the same time, you might want to consider giving samples to help promote your other products, if possible.

- Love – Connecting to the emotional side is quite important. Using words like happy or love will help potential customers get the same feeling viewing the product and really connect with them if they already feel that way.

- Delivered – It will arrive at my home safe and sound.

- Direct – No waiting period sounds amazing to many customers. So direct delivery is like a mega word for a lot of people.

- Immediately – If direct sounds too professional, immediate can be used as a positive replacement.

- Lifetime – Everyone wants something that'll last. Say you're selling a gift box for bridesmaids. You can list it as memorabilia for a lifetime's friendship. You're immediately connecting with your audience and showing them they're buying something worth their money.

- Results – If you're selling beauty, skin care or the like on Etsy, this word is your best friend. Everyone wants to know the benefits your custom made product will provide them and when. So, focus on the result when in such a category.

- Savings – Saving money is always a win for potential buyers, even if it's just through purchasing wisely. Give your customers the feel they're saving by purchasing your products whether through actual saving campaigns or using the quality of your product.

- Bargain – Same goes for a bargain, but it's something that amps up the intensity of your savings.

- How – How is the question on everyone's mind and answering it really helps them feel confident in their purchase.

- Hurry – Creates urgency and tells them they need to act fast.

- Offer – Suggests that this isn't a permanent arrangement.

Don't be afraid to use these common selling words, because they are subtle, and you'll see everyone using them. Not to mention, this is exactly what readers of your product descriptions want to hear.

Engage with your audience and get a sense of what they need from you to help them feel more confident when hitting that buy button.

Veronica McKinnon

Chapter 8

Getting Featured on Etsy

Etsy features a number of product listings on their homepage, and it's a much-coveted spot for many Etsy sellers. How could it not? You're appearing in Etsy emails, Etsy's blogs, and its homepage. It a lot of exposure and a lot of potential sales. It has to get you wondering "How can I get featured?"

To a certain extent, every shop and item has its own way to reach the top. But one thing's for sure. Etsy's editors pick items which drive traffic to their vintage marketplace. It rewards those who help them reach new heights and diversifies their audience and even their sellers. Basically, you need to be top tier and a fierce competitor in order to be featured. Beginners should strive but not run after this spot. It's something to look forward to and not tangle yourself in trying to achieve. That said, a good shop has a few practices Etsy looks forward to and loves to highlight.

Remember that selection processes differ by shop categories and even their tags. But we're going to look at some common qualities and characteristics that Etsy editors and merchandisers look for when choosing which product to highlight and feature. There are so many incredible, unique and creative shops on Etsy, standing on can be tough; but well worth it.

This will basically be an overview of all the important details of what we've learned so far, but your checklist to attain Etsy fame.

So, how can you get featured on Etsy?

Make your shop accessible to potential buyers

You need a bit of rep before you can be featured on Etsy. After all, if nobody knows who you are or how to find you, you can't really hope to win in a place in Etsy's elite team. So remember to use a search optimized (whether through Etsy's own search engine or external search engines, like Google, Bing or Yahoo) to make it easy to find your shop. Be as descriptive as possible and use a search engine optimized keyword in order to have a better ranking. Also, make sure you use all 13 available tags and select words and phrases Etsy users are likely to search for when looking for your item or something similar.

Be as visual as possible

Eye catching photography is another fast and efficient way to grab someone's attention and get more traffic. Chic, clean and editorial style pictures, similar to those found in high-end blogs or magazines, are preferable and make a strong impression on Etsy merchandisers and editors. You'll also pique interest for other users who are keen on buying your products, improving your standing and ability to get featured. So take pictures which are clean, crisp and in focus. Not too bright, but not too dark. In an enticing environment which shows off your product, but not in a cluttered mess which makes it difficult to pinpoint what you're trying to sell. You can even use seasonal selling points (such as adding some Christmas lights) to give Etsy some good promotional material for their themed trends and stories. Remember that Etsy has a forum where you can share, talk or read news about the website and be informed of everything related to it. That said, do remember professional images do not mean you necessarily need to spend hundreds investing in a camera. If you have reached this position and think you can improve, go for it. But your trusty phone camera will be able to achieve similar results without costing much either. And, there's always that creative brain of yours to improve quality using not so common ways.

Don't sell an item, sell a brand

Having a cohesive, consistent and recognizable brand is not only important for you to sell your products, but for Etsy to help you stand out. If you're trying to cater to everything under the sun, Etsy can't pinpoint what your brand personality is and how they can sell you to their wider audience. Instead building a brand identity helps you stand out in certain categories and is far more likely to get you featured, in and out of Etsy's marketplace. Etsy, after all, is looking for brands which sell their marketplace, not just single items.

Have a story

We've talked about engagement earlier, and that's exactly what Etsy's after as well. It's a personalized, homey website made for individuals who love the same. So getting featured means embodying exactly that. If you're just a bunch of products, there's nothing different about you than most other shoppers on Etsy - who can be just as creative, witty and talented. What distinguishes you from others is your story. While you shouldn't dive into a story in your product listing, your store's About should contain this information. It's able to convey to your potential buyers and Etsy editors that you're a person who has overcome adversity through the passion and talent you have. It's about creating a business which improves or enhances people's lives and doesn't just provide products for the sake of money. But to advance and share their skills and talent. A good way to understand what Etsy loves to see in an About page can be seen by going through and studying up the Seller Handbook, and really seeing the values, Etsy editors try to inspire.

Be inspiring with your story and don't just sell your products, sell your brand using the experiences you've gained. This is how Etsy really knows you're a good challenger and up to handle Etsy fame. Perhaps most of all: Be authentic. This is really a lovely group of passionate crafters, and authenticity is something they love and seek. So whatever you do, be as authentic in your wording as possible and really show Etsy editors what you're all about.

Sell high-quality products

What you sell is at the core of your business and Etsy in general. Spending time to develop a strong product portfolio, keeping it updated and fresh increase your likelihood of getting featured on the website. Keep improving your designs, packaging, products, and diversify if you like. Show your creative output in a cohesiveness manner and stay on trend with the latest Etsy fads--that's how you ensure your store is a success that Etsy editors want to feature on their website.

Be a role model for others

Spread the word that you're a force to be reckoned with by spreading your brand and the expertise you have. Being a role model for others and sharing the experiences you've learned helps you and fellow Etsy sellers improve the quality of the marketplace you all share. You can even write articles for Etsy and interact with their editor's first hand as you build your repute. However, remember you need to some cred in order to be taken seriously.

These were all must-do items when it comes to Etsy. They should not only allow you to get some good sales and build yourself as a brand but get featured and recognized on Etsy itself. That said, there are a few things you should avoid if you want to stay competitive and avoid any issues when it comes to getting featured.

First, don't try to imitate others. Believe in your creativity and your ability to figure things out. Imitation won't do you any good since Etsy wants to feature stores which can be authentic, real and original. Additionally, don't try to infringe on other seller's intellectual property. In the long run, it will cost you as first movers often get the advantage of tapping into an untapped market.

Secondly, fill your information clearly and fully. Don't leave any information out. The more solid information you have, the more reliable your words and products are. More buyers will be attracted to your products and you'll be able to get tons of free points in the getting featured jar. Any missing information would make your content seem a little bland and won't make you stand out from the crowd.

Lastly, avoid policy violations at all cost. While we've discussed a few dos and don'ts in this book, you might want to familiarize yourself with Etsy's pre-written Seller Policy and House Rules. Not to mention stay updated with the latest news posted by Etsy in their forums to avoid any problems. Etsy can change their policies at any moments so do remember to check for any changes.

Getting featured on Etsy is a lovely goal to have, and you're likely to get a lot of sales out to it; but remember, getting featured isn't everything, and your main goal should be to provide customers with what they want and have fun with the crafts you make.

Veronica McKinnon

Conclusion

Etsy is an online marketplace where people from across the globe can interact with each other and engage in the activities of buying and selling handmade crafts and goods and vintage items. You get to build and promote your brand as well.

Etsy can be used as a side hobby, to sell a few items here and there. If you want to take your Etsy business to the next level, though, and potentially make a living through your Etsy shop, then there are many, many things that you will need to learn and consider before you take that step. Marketing and promotion, taxes, intellectual property, legal limitations — these are serious topics, and all come into play when you start up an Etsy shop. But getting serious about your Etsy shop can be well worth it, and there are many resources available to support and assist you with getting started.

The biggest advantage to selling your products on Etsy is that it is created to be a true community, with members supporting each other, providing advice and guidance, and promoting each other's products. In this book, you will have read about the different ways in which the Etsy community provides support to its members, and the many free resources that are available to sellers.

You have learned about the process of opening your Etsy shop and the various decisions that need to be made to determine how you will market your shop and products. You have explored what products you will sell, and the many advertising and promotional strategies that you might want to implement to build your Etsy business. We also touched on the importance of complying with Etsy's policies for sellers; Etsy is able to succeed and support its buyers and sellers through the enforcement of these policies, which keep the community positive and supportive and help to avoid any legal issues.

By now you must be familiar with what Etsy is all about and how to go about setting up your shop on Etsy. Etsy can prove to be a great tool in the hands of those capable of making use of it, and using the tips and strategies outlined in this book will allow you to use that tool as effectively as possible. The information provided in this book will get you started on Etsy without any difficulty, and you can gain the success that you have always dreamed of by showing some patience.

Thank you once again for choosing this book. I hope that you found it interesting and that it has proven to be an informative read!

Veronica McKinnon

Printed in Great Britain
by Amazon